I0901872

LEARNING ABOUT THE HOLY SPIRIT

AN INTERACTIVE STUDY GUIDE FOR KIDS

MARY ERICKSON

Warner Press, Inc.
Warner Press and Warner Press logo are trademarks of Warner Press, Inc.

Learning about the Holy Spirit: An Interactive Study Guide for Kids
Written by Mary Erickson

Requests for information should be sent to:
Warner Press, Inc.
2902 Enterprise Drive
Anderson, IN 46013
www.warnerpress.org

Editors: Robin Loisch, Elizabeth Flinn
Cover by Curtis Corzine
Design and Layout by Karen Muilenburg
ISBN: 9781684345236
Printed in USA

TABLE OF CONTENTS

INTRODUCTION
(Part 1)

How to Use This Activity Book
(A Note to Parents and Teachers)

PURPOSE

The Bible holds the answers to our questions about the Holy Spirit, Third Person of the Trinity. As kids use *Learning about the Holy Spirit* as their study guide, they will grow in their understanding of who the Holy Spirit is and how He helps us live for Jesus. To those who believe in Jesus and accept Him as Savior, the Holy Spirit comes to lead, teach, and enable us to live God's way. He gives us power and special gifts that equip us to serve God and glorify Jesus. As we read and study the Bible, we will learn what the Holy Spirit did in the lives of believers long ago and what He does in our lives today.

BOOK ORGANIZATION

This book is divided into 20 chapters and is suitable for use in a variety of contexts: at home with your family, in Christian schools and homeschools, or in Sunday school and children's church. Parents and teachers can set their own pace.

Each chapter focuses on a biblical concept or characteristic of the Holy Spirit. Explanation is given to help kids understand the Trinity and the Holy Spirit's role in it. Specific examples of the Holy Spirit's work are drawn from both the Old and New Testaments. Scriptural truths are conveyed clearly so that kids can learn, remember, and apply biblical teaching to their lives.

Chapters are divided into sections so you can choose how much material you wish to cover at one sitting. Some puzzles and activities can be worked independently. The plays and stories can become an activity for individual, family, or classroom fun.

SUPPLIES NEEDED

Bibles

This book uses Scripture from several versions of the Bible: New International Version (NIV), New King James Version (NKJV), New International Reader's Version (NIrV), New Living Translation (NLT), and King James Version (KJV). The NIV will be the primary reference.

Ideally each child should have his or her own Bible. A variety of translations will make the lessons more interesting; however, exact puzzle answers will be found in the NIV and NKJV, primarily.

Colored Pencils

Children will be learning how to color-code Bible verses. Purchase quality colored pencils (soft lead) so Bible pages will not tear. One set of pencils per person is recommended for the greatest enjoyment and efficiency.

Bible Tags (optional, but helpful)

Tags with the Bible book names can be attached to the edge of the first page of each book in the child's Bible. They will help children to locate books more quickly. Tags are available at bookstores or through the Internet.

Yarn or Ribbon (optional)

Each student will need four pieces of narrow ribbon or yarn, 12–14" long. These will be used as bookmarks, dividing the Bible into five sections. Put the ribbons at these locations: 1 Kings 1, Proverbs 1, Matthew 1, Romans 1. Using four different ribbon colors will help children find Scriptures and learn general locations of the books of the Bible.

Pencil and Eraser

A quality eraser will remove colored pencil marks in the Bible.

Dictionary

Looking up words helps children learn their meanings. Writing them in the margin of the study manual helps with long-term memory.

Index Cards

Included in this study are several methods to help make memorizing scriptures easier and fun. Copying suggested verses on index cards helps in memorizing and in reviewing.

IDEAS FOR CONDUCTING THE SESSION

Atmosphere

Make your Bible study time a casual, happy experience. Sit around a table to provide closeness as well as a surface for writing and color-coding Bible verses. Be alert for waning attention of younger children. Don't require them to color-code all the verses or stay seated for the extended study meant to challenge older children. You might purchase coloring books to entertain those who cannot read so they can feel a part of this learning experience. The goal is to help children enjoy learning from the Bible.

Participation

Involvement is important. Let children assist in the planning. Everyone should have something to do at every session. Stress *cooperation* rather than *competition*, teamwork rather than rivalry. Let children participate according to their abilities.
Here are some suggestions:

1. Share events that happened or insights received since the last session.
2. Recite memorized verses.
3. Read the chapter title and key verse.
4. Share in reading the lesson or story. Become a character in a play.
5. Locate the Scripture verses.
6. Read the verse aloud as others follow along in their Bibles. If you have a variety of versions, let others read from their Bibles. Talk about different words used.
7. Discuss questions. Encourage everyone to participate. Be sensitive to children when they are willing to reveal their thoughts and feelings. This could develop into a time of open communication and an opportunity to understand each other. Never criticize.
8. Act as family or group recorder, filling in the blanks or completing an activity.
9. Color-code Bible verses with the proper colored pencils.
10. Read or create the closing prayer.
11. Watch for opportunities to praise one another.

Color-Coding Bible Verses

Color-coding is a simple method used to identify and mark selected subjects in the Bible. Most children enjoy this activity, but if you want to skip it, that's okay. It takes time but has some rich rewards.

Why color-code Bible verses?

1. It gives depth and purpose to Bible study. The reader must meditate on or analyze a verse to choose the proper color. Verses often require more than one color.
2. It helps the reader understand where basic topics are concentrated.
3. It enables the reader to select one subject for review during a meditation time.
4. It preserves years of study, making the Bible personal and precious to its owner.
5. It aids in memorizing verses and their references.

Planning Your First Session

In your first time together, provide an overview of what your child, family, or class will be doing in the coming chapters. The next section, "Getting Started," will take you step-by-step through this process.

Each child will learn according to his or her ability. If you provide the time and the opportunity, God will bless your efforts. Let the Holy Spirit be the teacher. Trust Him to speak to your children and reveal Jesus to them as you study together.

INTRODUCTION
(Part 2)

Getting Started
(A Note to Students)

INTRODUCING THE BOOK

In this activity book, you'll be learning about the Holy Spirit. You will discover who He is, what He does, and how He helps you live for Jesus.

You'll learn what the Holy Spirit did in people's lives long ago and how He still works in our lives today. You'll also have fun working puzzles, searching your Bible for answers, acting in plays, and reading stories. In the Discussion and Application sections, you will find questions to help you think or talk about some of your problems and some things you might not understand.

GETTING FAMILIAR WITH YOUR BIBLE

Understanding How the Bible Is Organized

The table of contents page is in the front of your Bible. In most Bibles, the books are listed in order from Genesis to Revelation. In others, the list is in alphabetical order. Page numbers are often given for each book of the Bible. This is a good place to look when you need help in locating an unfamiliar book.

The Bible is divided into two parts. The first part is called the Old Testament, and it is the story of God and His people. The second part is the New Testament, and it is the story of Jesus and His followers. The Old Testament has 39 books, and the New Testament has 27. The Bible has 66 books in all.

Sharing Unique Features

The Holy Bible is available in many different translations or versions. Look in the front of your Bible to see if you can identify which version or translation you have. Do you have pictures or maps? Do you have any charts or other study helps?

Locating the Colored Ribbons

A parent or teacher will give you four different colored ribbons. These will be bookmarks, dividing your Bible into five sections. Choose one color for each section. This will help you in locating Scripture verses later. Place a bookmark at 1 Kings 1, Proverbs 1, Matthew 1, and Romans 1.

COLOR-CODING YOUR BIBLE

One of the activities you will be doing is marking Bible verses with colored pencils. Color-coding a Bible verse will help you understand its meaning.

Coloring Hints

1. Color slowly and softly, so the pages won't tear.
2. Hold the pencil parallel to the page, tipping it slightly. Color with the side of the point, going back and forth several times.
3. Lay an index card at the sides of the verse. Coloring up to the card keeps the margins neat.

Choosing Your Color Code

First, you need to think about the colors you will use. It helps if the colors are selected meaningfully, in association with something—a symbol or emblem. Consider the suggestions below:

- **Purple**—royalty. The attributes of God: who God is, what He is like, what He has done.
- **Brown**—earth, reality. Duties and responsibilities of Christians: how we should act and speak.
- **Red**—blood. Jesus Christ: who He is and what He has done.
- **Blue**—sky. Anything about heaven, angels, or wisdom.
- **Green**—growing, alive. Holy Spirit: who He is and how He helps us.
- **Orange**—warmth, cheer. Family relationships: children, husbands, wives.
- **Yellow**—gold, valuable. Promises or rewards: what God will do for those who love and obey Him.

Making a Reference Card

To help remember the color code, use an index card to make a simplified version of the chart above (or colors chosen by you, your family, or group). Color each category on the card to create a handy reference.

On a larger card or on construction paper folded like a tent, print the books of the Bible with their common abbreviations. Place this "tent card" in the center of the table during each session so you can refer to it often.

Color-Coding a Verse

Let's color-code a few verses for practice.

1. Find John 14:26 in your Bible. Use your "tent card" or the table of contents in the front of your Bible if you need help.
2. Read the passage aloud.
3. Think about it. What does the verse say?
4. Decide what phrases should be color-coded. You don't have to color the entire verse.
5. Choose your colors thoughtfully. You might not always agree with other people.
6. If you follow the suggested colors in this book, you'll use the following pencils for John 14:26:
    - **Green**—*But the Advocate, the Holy Spirit,*
    - **Purple**—*who the Father will send in my name,*
    - **Green**—*will teach you all things and will remind you*
    - **Red**—*of everything I have said to you.*

7. If you want to color-code other passages, find these verses:
    - Romans 15:13 (purple, green)
    - Acts 1:8 (green, brown)
    - 1 Corinthians 6:19–20 (brown, green, purple, brown)

1

The Trinity

Memory Verse: Therefore go and make disciples of all nations, baptizing them in the name of the Father and of the Son and of the Holy Spirit.

MATTHEW 28:19 (NIV)

WHAT IS THE TRINITY?

The title of this book is *Learning about the Holy Spirit*. The Holy Spirit is the Third Person of the Trinity.

Have you wondered what or who the Trinity (with a capital T) is? Great preachers of the past have called the Trinity a mystery because it is hard to explain. This chapter will be an elementary introduction to this heavenly subject.

Remember when you were in first grade? Did your teacher give you a 200-page novel to read? No, of course not! You started with an easy reader that had several words on each page. I remember my first reader. The story was about a boy named Dick. It started out with these words:

Dick. See Dick. See Dick run.
Run, Dick, run!

In this chapter, we will begin by learning the basics about the Trinity, so we can discover who the Holy Spirit is. Then we can dive into this book to learn how the Holy Spirit helps us live for Jesus.

Definition and Earthly Examples

A simple definition of *trinity* (with a small t) is "a group of three people or things." Can you think of any groups of three?

"Three Blind ____________" or "Three Little ____________." Could each be labeled as a trio, a threesome, or a trinity?

In math, what shape has three sides? ______________________

If a mother has three babies at the same time, what do we call them? __________________

Could they be called a trinity?

Trinity in the Bible

But we want to talk about what Trinity with a capital T means. The word *Trinity* is not in the Bible, but the three Persons that it refers to are mentioned together many times. They are <u>God the Father</u>, <u>Jesus the Son of God</u>, and the <u>Holy Spirit</u>.

Read the Bible verses. Then fill in the blanks.

1. Apostle Paul wrote about three Persons in 2 Corinthians 13:14 (NIV).

   "May the grace of the __________ ____________ ____________, and the love of __________, and the ______________________ of the __________ ____________ be with you all."

2. Dr. Luke mentioned the three Persons in Luke 3:21b–22 (NIV).

   "As he [Jesus] was praying, __________________ was opened and the __________ __________ descended on him in bodily form like a __________. And a ____________ came from heaven: 'You are _______ _________, whom I love; with you I am well ______________.'"

3. Jesus mentioned the three Persons in Matthew 28:19 (NIV), when He gave the Great Commission to His disciples.

   "Therefore go and make disciples of all nations, baptizing them in the name of the ________________ and of the ________ and of the _________ ____________."

Christians believe there is only One True God. This One God, by His very divine nature, exists in three Persons—Father, Son, and Holy Spirit. This is the mystery that is hard to understand. The concept of the Trinity is a belief that we must accept by faith.

ILLUSTRATIONS OF THE TRINITY

Preachers have used nature and other images to help explain the Trinity—One God with three Persons who each have God's nature within them.

How can there be three in one? Here are some earthly examples to think about:

- An egg has three parts: the shell, the white, and the yolk.
- Water has three different forms: liquid, solid, and steam.
- Rebecca is a woman we read about in the Old Testament. She was a daughter of Laban, a wife of Isaac, and a mother of Jacob and Esau—all at the same time. But she was only one person.

A Green Example

Did you ever wear green on March 17 for St. Patrick's Day?

Saint Patrick was a Christian missionary to the people of Ireland during the fourth century. To teach non-believers about the Trinity, he used the shamrock as a training tool. The shamrock is a three-leaf clover, common in Ireland.

Saint Patrick talked about this small plant with three leaves growing on one stem. The stem that holds them all together represents The Triune God. The three leaves represent the Father, the Son, and the Holy Spirit.

For centuries, many artists drew this as a symbol for the Trinity. Here is one example.

Hymns about the Trinity

1. Reginald Heber, an English bishop and poet, wrote "Holy, Holy, Holy!" Years later in 1861, John Dykes composed the tune. It was declared to be one of the finest hymns ever written. Perhaps you have sung it in church many times. Here is Verse Four:

Holy, holy, holy! Lord God Almighty!
All Thy works shall praise Thy name,
in earth and sky and sea;
Holy, holy, holy! merciful and mighty!
God in three Persons, blessed Trinity!

2. In 1674, Thomas Ken wrote a song that you may have sung often at the close of morning worship on Sunday. It is called the Doxology.

Praise God, from whom all blessings flow;
Praise Him, all creatures here below;
Praise Him above, ye heavenly host;
Praise Father, Son, and Holy Ghost. Amen.

CHALLENGE

Paul's Prayer for Believers

These Bible verses from Paul's letter to the Ephesians show how God, Jesus, and the Holy Spirit are interconnected. Circle the underlined words from this Scripture in the puzzle below. Words may be found forwards, backwards, up, down, or diagonally.

"For this reason I kneel before the Father,
from whom every family in heaven and on earth derives its name.
I pray that out of his glorious riches he may strengthen you
with power through his Spirit in your inner being,
so that Christ may dwell in your hearts through faith."

Ephesians 3:14–17 (NIV)

```
A L P R T R F T F N X M G X D S U G T V D W V C S
A H I N P B R D T J V H L Z H T R A E R K K X T A
K V T U L H C F Q X E U O X G E Z E E U M D R N L
A R E N N I V S E A U X R D T L F A P Z W E A S H
I O C L L N K W V I L G I K T O S N X E N E I W H
F M H W P K D E R H Q S O B C O L K L G R H M E W
S H R I T W N I Q Z P C U K N I Q L T H X G A V S
X K I C N F Y J Z C F K S X T A C H W R O R Y N R
E I S B R T F R C O D G N C D K E T W G T U Y K H
Z S T U J V E T Z G I I Z C Q N M G N S H Z N L K
I S O X D W Y D G M W V A Z B B M I T X K O L S Q
V Y W A O L B C D D O U R H X R E X L F J J B K N
Z N F P X N H J M M N M B G E B W J A I Z U F U G
L G Z K T L U I A O D K K L Q P Q Q F H T M Y J S
M Y E M W Q P S I W S D O T Y L A I I L E E N K Z
W O J R D L N Q Y N J A I S D O Y L A H A T E S U
B N Y Y W J D X P V G R Y Q N W U A V F U R E N V
O E K E M P A C Y Y I T U Q B A U S E H C I R T F
E B E F O R E R C P N I L G J O I N X P N X C A G
M H Q N E E E E S M M Y D F K H X S F S H I M F B
A D Z V S Q T H R O U G H V C C H F E T W I M M E
N Q P O Z X N T N G H P G M A V C V I H L V M G F
M A R B L X Z A B J G Q V M M L K A U Y P Y O S X
W H O M N E R F F P S G G X V I F D Z N E E B Y I
```

Answers on page 121

DISCUSSION

1. What do you think of the term "heavenly family" for the Trinity?
2. Share what you have learned. What questions do you still have?

APPLICATION

1. As you read Ephesians 3:14–17 about the Trinity again, use your colored pencils to color-code the verses in your Bible. You'll need purple for God the Father, red for Jesus Christ the Son, green for the Holy Spirit or Holy Ghost [Advocate, Helper, Comforter, Counsellor], and brown for your responsibilities. This can be fun! You will also be able to find these verses again easily in your Bible when you need encouragement.
2. A Verse to Memorize. Copy the verse below on an index card. Underline or print important words (shown in bold print) in color to help you remember the verse. You may want to color-code this verse in your Bible as well.

This is how we ***know*** *that we* ***live*** *in him and he in us:*
He [God] *has* ***given*** *us of his* ***Spirit****.*
And we have seen and ***testify*** *that the* ***Father***
has sent his ***Son*** *to be the* ***Savior*** *of the* ***world****.*

1 John 4:13–14 (NIV), emphasis added

PRAYER

Heavenly Father,
Your name is holy, and Your deeds are mighty.
I want to use words from the Doxology in my prayer.
I acknowledge and praise God from whom all blessings flow.
I praise God along with all creatures here below
and all the angels in heaven.
I worship the Father, Son, and Holy Spirit.
I am grateful for learning about the Trinity.
Please help me, God, to grow in understanding and faith.
In the precious name of Jesus, I pray. Amen.

2

The Promise

Memory Verse: Very truly I tell you, it is for your good that I am going away. Unless I go away, the Advocate *[Helper]* will not come to you; but if I go, I will send him to you.

JOHN 16:7 (NIV)

For three years, the disciples had walked and worked with Jesus. They watched Him perform many miracles: heal the sick, raise the dead, cast out devils, calm the seas, and feed the crowds. Jesus had been their teacher, trainer, friend, and counselor.

PROMISE MADE

Before His crucifixion, Jesus told His disciples He was going to leave them and go back to His Father in heaven. The disciples were sad and confused. This did not make sense to them. Jesus was their leader. What would they do without Him?

Then Jesus spoke tenderly to them and made a promise.
Read the Bible verses. Then fill in the blanks.

1. John 14:15–18 (NIV). "If you ________ me, keep my ________________. And I will ________ the _______________, and he will give you another ______________ to ________ you and be with you ________________ — the ___________ of ___________.... I will not leave you as ______________."

2. John 14:26–27 (NIV). Jesus repeated His promise. "The _______________, the _________ ____________, whom the Father will send in my ___________, will ____________ you all things and will _________________ _________ of _____________________________ I have said to you. _____________ I leave with you; my peace I give __________."

3. Acts 1:4, 8 (NIV). Later, before Jesus ascended to heaven, He reminded the apostles of His promise once more. "Do not leave ________________, but wait for the ________ my Father ______________, which you have heard me __________ about.... You will receive ____________ when the ________ __________ comes on you; and you will be my ____________________ in Jerusalem, and in all __________ and Samaria, and to the ________ of the __________."

PROMISE KEPT

Just as Jesus had promised, the Holy Spirit came on the day of Pentecost. About 120 of Jesus' followers were waiting together in one place. Miracles happened when the Holy Spirit came. Read Acts 2:1–13 (NIV) to find out what happened. Then complete the puzzle.

Day of Pentecost

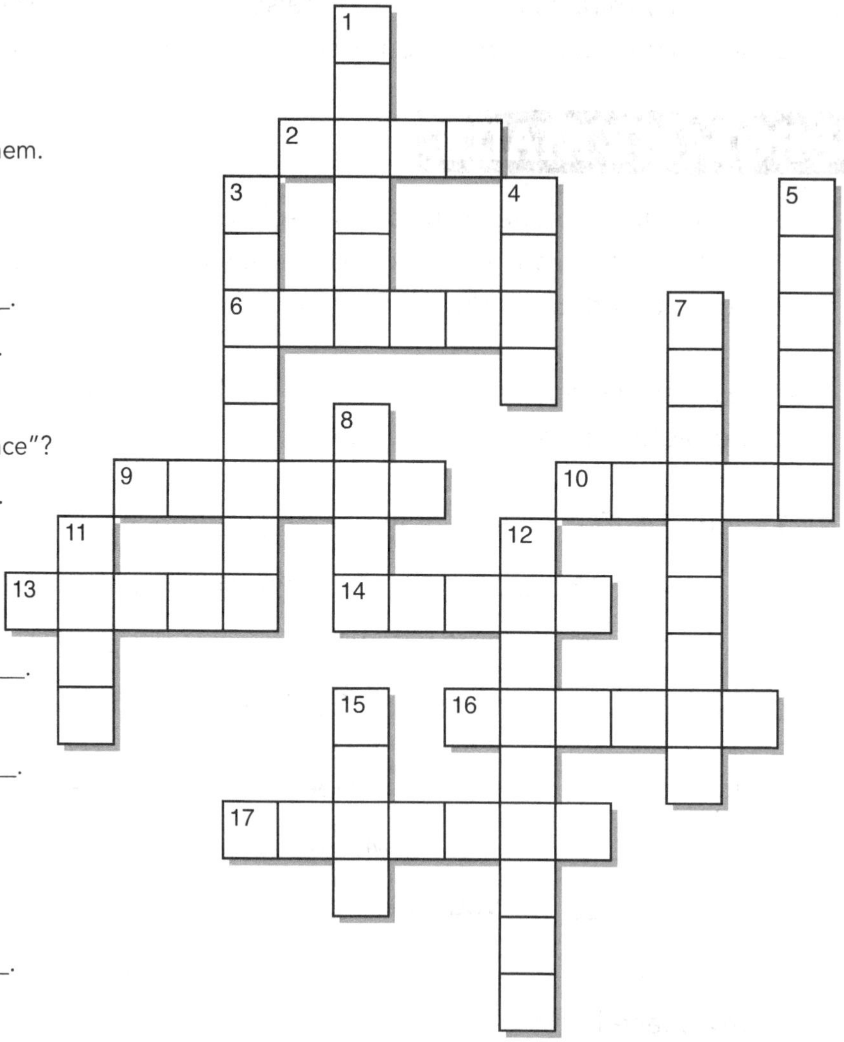

Across

2. Flames of ___rested on each of them.
6. The people were from every ___.
9. The wind came from ___.
10. Suddenly the people heard a ___.
13. The people were sitting in a ___.
14. Another word for talk is ___.
16. What word means "no more space"?
17. The disciples spoke in other ___.

Down

1. People were filled with the Holy ___.
3. Everyone heard their own ___.
4. They heard a violent or rushing ___.
5. Some people were ___.
7. This event took place in ___.
8. People at this event were all ___.
11. A word that describes God is ___.
12. The speakers were all ___.
15. People mocked and said disciples drank ___.

Answers on page 121

GETTING ACQUAINTED WITH THE HOLY SPIRIT

You have learned that the Holy Spirit is an important member of the Trinity: God the Father, Jesus the Son, and the Holy Spirit. When Jesus went back to heaven, He sent the Holy Spirit to take His place. The Holy Spirit would be the teacher to His disciples and to all believers. You will learn more in this book about the ministry of the Holy Spirit. 1) What did He do in New Testament times? 2) What are His main jobs in the lives of believers today?

Your First Meeting

Do you remember when you first heard about the Holy Spirit? Maybe you are hearing about Him for the first time right now. One of the first times in the New Testament where the Holy Spirit is mentioned is in the Christmas story about the birth of Jesus. Let's review those facts.

The Holy Spirit and Mary, the Mother of Jesus

Use the reference to find the verse in your Bible. Then draw the picture from Column 1 beside the correct verse in Column 2.

REFERENCE	WORDS OF PROOF
Matthew 1:22–23 (NIV) 	*"This is how the birth of Jesus the Messiah came about: His mother Mary was pledged to be married to Joseph, but before they came together, she was found to be pregnant through the Holy Spirit."*
Luke 1:35 (NIV) 	*"Therefore the Lord himself will give you a sign: The virgin will conceive and give birth to a son, and will call him Immanuel."*
Matthew 1:18 (NIV) 	*"Joseph son of David, do not be afraid to take Mary home as your wife, because what is conceived in her is from the Holy Spirit."*
Isaiah 7:14 (NIV) 	*"The angel answered, 'The Holy Spirit will come on you, and the power of the Most High will overshadow you. So the holy one to be born will be called the Son of God.'"*
Mathew 1:20 (NIV) 	*"All this took place to fulfill what the Lord had said through the prophet: 'The virgin will conceive and give birth to a son, and they will call him Immanuel' (which means 'God with us')."*

Answers on page 121

DISCUSSION

Jesus promised that the Holy Spirit would come to help the disciples, and that's exactly what happened.

1. Do you think the disciples had a hard time believing Jesus would keep His promise? Why or why not?
2. Can people trust you to keep your promises? If not, how can you do better?
3. What emotions do you think the believers felt on the day of Pentecost? Think or talk about what the non-believers might have thought. How would you explain to them what happened?

APPLICATION

1. Have you ever thought about keeping a journal?
   In a journal, you write your own personal thoughts and feelings about things that happened—both happy and sad. How did you feel when you had a fight with a friend? Or when you were successful in something? Writing can be a healing process or help you solve a problem. Maybe you would like to write about your spiritual journey and how you are learning more about God, Jesus, and the Holy Spirit. Be sure to date each entry.
2. A Verse to Memorize. Copy the verse below on an index card. Underline or print important words (shown in bold print) in color to help you remember the verse. You may want to color-code this verse in your Bible as well.

If you ***love*** *me, keep my* ***commands****.*
And I will ***ask*** *the* ***Father****,*
and he will ***give*** *you another* ***advocate*** [comforter]
to ***help*** *you and be with you* ***forever****—the* ***Spirit*** *of* ***truth****.*

John 14:15–17 (NIV), emphasis added

PRAYER

Today, take this time to write your own prayer.

- Open your prayer with praise to God for who He is and what He has done. You could use a Psalm (Example: 18:1–2) or a hymn (Example: "Great Is Thy Faithfulness") to begin your prayer.
- Thank God for all He has done for you, your family, or friends.
- Request help for your family and friends.
- Then make your needs known to the Heavenly Father.
- Tell God about your own dreams, plans, or goals.
- Express your love and thanks to God.
- Close your prayer with words like these: In the name of Jesus, I pray. Amen.

3

The Holy Spirit Lives in You

Memory Verse: *[Jesus said,]* "I will ask the Father and he will give you another advocate to help you and be with you forever—the Spirit of truth.... You know him, for he lives with you and will be in you."

JOHN 14:16–17 (NIV)

Close your eyes and picture in your mind past Christmas trees. Can you see the shining lights and the bright red balls? Or were they gold or blue? Can you see those colorful packages under the tree? When no one was watching, did you sneak about examining them to see which ones had your name on the tag?

Think about the mornings or evenings when everyone gathered and opened those presents. What do you remember as one of the best gifts you ever received?

____

____

____

____

GIFTS FROM GOD

One of God's greatest gifts was His Son, *Jesus Christ*, who He sent to earth as a baby. Jesus came to save us from our sins.

To those who accept His Son, God gave another gift—*eternal life.*
Read the Bible verse. Then fill in the blanks.

John 3:16 (NIV). "For God so ____________ the world that he __________ his one and only Son, that whoever _________________in him shall not _____________ but have _______________ life."

But wait. That's not all. God also gave another wonderful gift—His *Holy Spirit.* As believers, we received the Holy Spirit the moment we confessed our sins and accepted Jesus Christ as the Son of God.

How do we know that for sure?

THE HOLY SPIRIT LIVES AND WORKS IN BELIEVERS

The Holy Spirit helps us to know when we have sinned and disobeyed God. He gives us power to live a holy life and strengthens our desire to do things God's way.

Read the Bible verses. Then fill in the blanks.

Ephesians 1:13 (NIV). Paul wrote: "You also were included in Christ when you heard the message of truth, the gospel of your ___________________. When you believed, you were marked in him with a seal, the promised _________ _____________."

Acts 2:38 (NIV). Peter preached: "Repent and be baptized, every one of you, in the name of Jesus Christ for the _______________________ of your sins. And you will receive the _______ of the _________ _____________."

1 John 4:13, 15 (NIV). John wrote: "This is how we know that we live in him and he in us: He has given us of his ___________.... If anyone ________________________ that Jesus is the Son of God, God ___________ in __________ and __________ in God."

The Bible says you are God's temple. In the Old Testament, King Solomon built a temple to honor God. Sometimes we call a church the "house of God." We know that God doesn't live inside a building, but we honor God by going there to worship and learn about Him. When you accept Jesus as your Savior, your body becomes like a temple for God because you want to honor Him with your life. His Holy Spirit is in you.

1 Corinthians 3:16 (NIV). "Don't you know that you yourselves are ____________ ________________ and that _________ ________________ dwells in your midst?"

1 Corinthians 6:19–20 (NIV). "Do you not know that your bodies are ______________ of the Holy Spirit, who is in you, whom you have received from _________? You are not your own; you were bought _________ ____ _____________. Therefore __________ God with _________ ______________."

HOW CAN YOU HONOR GOD?

Read Galatians 5:13–18, 25 (NIV) and find six statements that show ways that we can honor God. Write the phrases that start with verbs (action words). The first letter has been given to help you.

1. Verse 13. **S** ________________________________

2. Verse 14. **L** ________________________________

3. Verse 16. **W** ________________________________

4. Verse 18. **L** ________________________________

5. Verse 25. **L** ________________________________

6. Verse 25. **K** ________________________________

In Galatians 5:19–21, Paul lists some sinful actions. He warned that people who live like this will not inherit eternal life. BUT, in contrast, he lists the fruit of the Holy Spirit. These nine qualities of Jesus are produced in a believer's life as we learn and grow in our knowledge of Him. You'll discover these fruits in the following puzzle.

Answers on page 121

CHALLENGE

Nine Fruits of the Spirit: Part 1

To solve this double-digit code:

1. Select the first number (digit) in the GRAY COLUMN on the left.
2. Using the BLACK ROW on the top, find the second number (digit).
3. Where the column and row meet will be the letter for the puzzle below.

Example 41 is 4+1 = P

	1	2	3	4	5
1	A	B	C	D	E
2	F	G	H	I	J
3	K	L	M	N	O
4	P	Q	R	S	T
5	U	V	W	X	Y

1. P ___ ___ ___ ___
   41 15 11 13 15

2. ___ ___ ___ ___ ___ ___ ___ ___ ___ ___
   22 15 34 45 32 15 34 15 44 44

3. ___ ___ ___ ___
   32 35 52 15

4. ___ ___ ___ ___ ___ ___ ___ ___
   31 24 34 14 34 15 44 44

5. ___ ___ ___
   25 35 55

6. ___ ___ ___ ___ ___ ___ ___ ___ ___ ___ ___ ___
   21 11 24 45 23 21 51 32 34 15 44 44

Answers on page 121

Nine Fruits of the Spirit: Part 2

To solve this double-digit code:

1. Select the first number (digit) in the GRAY COLUMN on the left.
2. Using the BLACK ROW on the top, find the second number (digit).
3. Where the column and row meet will be the letter for the puzzle below.

   Example 44 is 4+4 = S

	1	2	3	4	5
1	A	B	C	D	E
2	F	G	H	I	J
3	K	L	M	N	O
4	P	Q	R	S	T
5	U	V	W	X	Y

7. S___ ___ ___ – ___ ___ ___ ___ ___ ___ ___
44 15 32 21 13 35 34 45 43 35 32

8. ___ ___ ___ ___ ___ ___ ___ ___
22 35 35 14 34 15 44 44

Three choices for #9 from three different Bible versions.

9a. ___ ___ ___ ___ ___ ___ ___ ___ ___ ___ ___ **(NIV)**
21 35 43 12 15 11 43 11 34 13 15

9b. ___ ___ ___ ___ ___ ___ ___ ___ ___ ___ ___ ___ ___ **(NKJV)**
32 35 34 22 44 51 21 21 15 43 24 34 22

9c. ___ ___ ___ ___ ___ ___ ___ ___ **(NLT)**
41 11 45 24 15 34 13 15

From: ___ ___ ___ ___ ___ ___ ___ ___ ___ **5:22–23**
22 11 32 11 45 24 11 34 44

DISCUSSION

1. How would you define *faithfulness, goodness, gentleness*?
2. How would you define *forbearance*? You may want to look it up in a dictionary. How can you develop that fruit?

Answers on page 121

APPLICATION

1. What can you do to make the Fruit of the Spirit a part of your life? Make a chart to post in your room so you can be reminded of what they are.
2. Choose one fruit that you want to start developing in your life.
3. A Verse to Memorize. Copy the verse below on an index card. Underline or print important words (shown in bold print) in color to help you remember the verse. You may want to color-code this verse in your Bible as well.

Do you not know that
your ***bodies*** *are* ***temples*** *of the* ***Holy Spirit****,*
who is ***in*** *you, whom you have* ***received*** *from God?*
You are not your ***own****; you were* ***bought*** *at a* ***price****.*
Therefore ***honor*** *God with your* ***bodies****.*

1 Corinthians 6:19–20 (NIV), emphasis added

PRAYER

(Start with Matthew 6:9–10 NIV.)

"Our Father in heaven,
hallowed be your name,
your kingdom come, your will be done,
on earth as it is in heaven."

Dear God,
You are filled with loving kindness.
Thank You for the blessings You give to my family.
I pray that (name these people) *will know about Your love.*
Thank You for sending the Holy Spirit to live in me
and to teach me how to live a life that pleases You.
I ask all this in the precious name of Jesus. Amen.

4

The Holy Spirit Shows No Favoritism

Memory Verse: God does not show favoritism but accepts from every nation the one who fears him and does what is right.

ACTS 10:34–35 (NIV)

Have you ever known someone who was the "teacher's pet"? That student was chosen for special jobs like room monitor or line leader. Maybe the teacher praised him or her in front of the class for getting good grades.

Pretty soon, the other students noticed that he or she was the teacher's favorite. Students who were not chosen or praised began to feel bad. Some of them felt sad, mad, or jealous that one student got extra attention.

God does not choose favorites. The Holy Spirit wants every person to know Jesus and have a close relationship with Him.

The Holy Spirit Directs

After Jesus returned to heaven, the disciples continued Jesus' ministry. They taught the Jews the truth about God and about who Jesus is. God planned for the gospel to be shared with the Gentiles as well. This was hard for the disciples to understand at first. They believed only the Jews were special to God. They thought the Gentiles did not honor or worship God in the right way.

Soon, Peter was going to see the Holy Spirit in action. Peter was going to find out that the Holy Spirit was sent for both Jews *and* Gentiles.

READ A PLAY

This play shows how the Holy Spirit spoke to men several times, according to God's will. If you are reading this play with a small group, one person can read all three parts marked with an *.

Peter Obeys the Spirit

From Acts 10 and 11

CAST:
- **Narrator**—storyteller who describes the action and setting
- **Peter**—apostle of Jesus
- **Cornelius**—Roman army officer; a godly Gentile
- **Angel***—God's messenger
- **Voice***—heavenly speaker
- **Holy Spirit***—God's Helper
- **Soldier**—member of the group of men Cornelius sent

Scene 1—Home of Cornelius in Caesarea

Narrator: Cornelius was a Roman Centurion who lived in Caesarea. He was a God-fearing man who prayed regularly and gave generously to the poor. The Jews called him "an outsider" because he was a Gentile. One afternoon he had a vision. He saw an angel of God coming toward him.

Angel: Cornelius!

Cornelius: What is it, Lord?

Angel: Your prayers and gifts to the poor have come up as a memorial offering before God. Now send men to Joppa to bring back a man named Simon Peter. He is staying with Simon the tanner, whose house is by the sea.

Narrator: After the angel left, Cornelius called a trusted soldier and two servants. He told them what had just happened. Then he sent them to Joppa.

Scene 2—The home of Simon the tanner in Joppa

Narrator: About noon on the next day, Peter went up on the roof to pray. While waiting for his meal to be served, he had a vision.

Narrator: The clouds parted in the sky, and a large canvas sheet dropped down to earth by its four corners. It was bulging with four-footed animals like pigs and rabbits, crawling creatures like snakes and snails, and birds like crows and hawks.

Voice: Get up, Peter! Kill and eat!

Peter: No! Never! Not me! The Hebrew laws forbid us Jews to eat such unclean animals.

Voice: Don't argue with God, Peter. Do not call anything polluted or dirty that God has made clean.

Narrator: The same vision was repeated three times. Then the sheet was pulled back into the heavens.

Peter: *(shaking head)* I am so confused. What does this mean? I can't make any sense out of it. What am I supposed to do?

Narrator: Just then Peter heard strange voices coming from the front gate.

Soldier: Is there a man living here whose name is Simon Peter?

Narrator: Peter was still thinking about the vision and its possible meaning when the Holy Spirit interrupted his thoughts.

Holy Spirit: Simon, there are three men downstairs searching for you. Go down and meet them. Go with them. Do not doubt nor delay because I have sent them.

Narrator: Peter hurried down to meet the strangers.

Peter: I am Peter, the man you are looking for. What do you want?

Soldier: Our master Cornelius sent us. He is a Roman Centurion, a righteous and God-fearing man. He is good and honest, respected by the Jews. A holy angel told him to invite you to come to his house so that he could hear your message. He wants to learn what God wants him to do.

Narrator: Peter invited the three men in to be his guests and gave them lodging for the night. The next day Peter went with them to Caesarea. A few friends from Joppa went along.

Scene 3—The home of Cornelius in Caesarea

Narrator: Cornelius had gathered his family and friends into his house to meet with Peter. When Peter arrived, Cornelius knelt at his feet in worship. Peter reached out and helped him to his feet.

Peter: Stand up, man. I am not a god. I'm just a human being like you.

Narrator: After getting acquainted, they went inside the house. Peter met the people and then began to speak.

Peter: You know that I am a Jew. It is against the Jewish laws for me to mingle with Gentiles or to come into a home like this. But God has shown me that I should never think of anyone as inferior or beneath me. So, I came quickly and willingly. Now please tell me why you invited me here.

Cornelius: A few days ago, I was in my house praying as usual. Suddenly, a man clothed in a splendid robe stood before me. He said, "Cornelius, your prayer has been heard. Your gifts to the poor have been seen by God. Send to Joppa for Simon Peter who lives in the home of Simon the tanner by the seaside."

So, I sent for you at once. Now we are all here in the presence of God to listen to what the Lord has commanded you to tell us.

Peter: Now I realize how true it is that God does not show favoritism. He accepts people from every nation who fear Him and do what is right.

You have heard about the baptism that John preached and how God anointed Jesus of Nazareth with the Holy Spirit and power. You have also heard how Jesus went about doing good and healing the sick and all who were possessed by demons, for God was with Him.

Narrator: Cornelius and his family all nodded in agreement. Peter continued with the gospel message.

Peter: We disciples are witnesses of all that Jesus preached and did. We can testify that the people killed Him by hanging Him on a cross.

But God raised Him on the third day, and Jesus was seen by many of His followers. He commanded us to preach that everyone who believes in Him will receive forgiveness of sins through His name.

Narrator: While Peter was still speaking, the Holy Spirit came on all who heard the message. They began praising God and speaking in other languages. The friends from Joppa were amazed that the gift of the Holy Spirit had been poured out on the Gentiles.

The day ended with the new believers being baptized in the name of the Lord Jesus.

—THE END—

Soon word spread to the apostles and other believers in Judea about what had happened at Cornelius' house. When Peter returned to Jerusalem, they criticized him for befriending Gentiles and spending time with them.

Peter explained everything that had happened. He told them how God had spoken to him, how the Gentiles believed in Jesus, and how the Holy Spirit came upon them.

A Change of Heart

Read Acts 11:15–18 to see what Peter said about his change of heart and how the Jews responded to him. Then circle these words from the Bible passage. Words may be hidden forwards, backwards, up, down, or diagonally.

Speak	**Holy Spirit**	**Beginning**	**Remembered**
Lord	**John**	**Baptized**	**Water**
God	**Gift**	**Gave**	**Believed**
Jesus	**Think**	**Stand**	**Objections**
Praised	**Gentiles**	**Granted**	**Repentance**

D B V S O Y H R Y E G Y H N B Q L W P V M C L D G
E U W M B C S X Q L F O C Y V M D N B P F G Y J M
O X A S X A I Z C B L S M Y O C V V J I D N A T S
W J T Y F D P E U Y E X R R X H S N S G M B N H U
K B E G R K T T S N R X E O J L L Q S W T K A I R
S C R O E G U P I E F M R F J O E Z B N B L P N P
D G L C S U I Y A Z E X T B E E S G C T A B D P Q
Y Q I E E R K Y O M E A P O E C B A R H O K P O P
K Z N F I D D D B Q G D X R F Q N A D I F F J R G
V D T T T Y B E A C V O O Y F M F A K N Z O A I W
S D P D W A R Z V M J I J A R S C W T K Z I J E L
N O G P Y E D B Y X K G Z E I R C M T N S W L N X
O E C Q D Z M C G Z N A W D T J P R W E E A P W N
I J X K X G D I N I V S Z E N T N G D U D P G Z C
T Y S P N G R A N T E D R V G Q X F K C Y S E H O
C W W O E K E N G B B F F E C H S C M K P K R R H
E N X R P L I Z L C Z S Q I Z B U Q N E T N M V P
J R P M I G O L F U V Y P L N C S F A W I S H Z W
B Z Q Y E O P Z E A X U U E X F E K F I H V Z O L
O D I B G E N T I L E S H B R C J Z Z E V A G P J

Answers on page 121

DISCUSSION

1. Talk about how and to whom the Holy Spirit spoke.
2. Have you had special guidance in the past, but did not know it might have been the Holy Spirit? Share about it or write about it in your journal.

APPLICATION

1. Read Acts 10 and 11. Color-code verses about the Holy Spirit in green and Acts 10:34–35 in purple for God.
2. A Verse to Memorize. Copy the verse below on an index card. Underline or print important words (shown in bold print) in color to help you remember the verse.

God** does **not** show **favoritism
*but **accepts** from every **nation***
*the one who **fears** him*
*and **does** what is **right**.*

Acts 10:34–35 (NIV), emphasis added

*Note the words *fears him* in the verse above. This phrase means "trusts or honors God." Read the verse again and substitute the new meaning.

PRAYER

Dear Heavenly Father,
Everything You do is right and fair.
I'm so glad that You accept people
of every color and country.
Thanks for sending Your Holy Spirit
to show me the way to treat other people.
Some of my classmates are from other lands.
Forgive me, Lord, for not always treating them fairly.
Remind me to be fair and kind to others
on the playground, in sports, and at home.
I pray that You will help my family today. (Name them and tell why.)
In the precious name of Jesus, amen.

5

The Holy Spirit Is the Comforter

Memory Verse: I will pray the Father,
and he shall give you another Comforter,
that he may abide with you for ever.

JOHN 14:16 (KJV)

A SUBSTITUTE IS COMING

School is wonderful! It's so much fun. You have been enjoying the best teacher you have ever had. Then one day she says, "I am not going to be your teacher any longer. You will have a substitute to take my place beginning tomorrow."

How would you feel? Perhaps heartbroken and confused just like the disciples felt when Jesus told them He was leaving. Jesus told them, "I am going back to my Father who sent me. But I will send a Comforter to take my place."

WHAT IS A COMFORTER?

A *comforter* is a helper who stays by our side to give aid in times of trouble. A comforter can also relieve our distress and give us calm and cheer.

Who or What Is a Comforter to You?

When you are having a hard time, where do you find comfort?

Some situations and possible comforters are described below. Draw a line from each event in "A Time of Trouble" to the correct "Comforter."

A Time of Trouble	Comforter
You are cold at night.	Hugging your favorite teddy bear or pet can make you glad.
You are sick and your stomach aches.	Your teacher can explain the problem.
You are sad.	You crawl under a thick blanket filled with fluffy stuff that warms you.
You are lonely.	Mother cleans the cut and puts on a bandage.
You are hurt and bleeding.	The doctor can make you feel better.
Your schoolwork is hard.	A friend can fill the empty feeling.

Jesus gave the name *Comforter* to the Holy Spirit. The original King James Version (KJV) was first published in 1611. This Bible uses the word *Comforter* as the name of the Holy Spirit. However, in 1982, a New King James Version (NKJV) was published. That version and other popular Bibles use the word *Helper, Advocate*, or *Counselor* in place of Comforter. In this chapter, we will use the KJV Bible.

REASONS WHY JESUS SENT THE COMFORTER

1. To take His place.

> *"I will pray the Father, and he shall give you another Comforter, that he may abide with you for ever; Even the Spirit of truth.... I will not leave you comfortless."* John 14:16–18 (KJV)

Now copy this verse from your Bible on the lines below. Note the word substituted for Comforter. Color-code the words that describe the Holy Spirit in green.
Underline the new word.

____

____

____

____

Answers on page 121

Notice the word *another*. Jesus had been the disciples' Comforter. Now God was going to send *another* Comforter to take Jesus' place.

2. To teach them all things and to remind them of what Jesus said.

> *"The Comforter, which is the Holy Ghost, whom the Father will send in my name, he shall teach you all things, and bring all things to your remembrance, whatsoever I have said unto you."* John 14:26 (KJV)

Copy this verse from your Bible.

____

____

____

Have you ever wondered how the Gospel writers could remember the exact words Jesus spoke, and where and how He performed so many miracles?

Now you know! The Holy Spirit helped the disciples remember all the words and works of Jesus when they were writing the New Testament. Peter, one of Jesus' closest disciples, proved this when he wrote:

> *"No prophecy of the Scripture is of any private interpretation, for prophecy never came by the will of man, but holy men of God spoke as they were moved by the Holy Spirit."* 2 Peter 1:20–21 (NJKV)

3. To testify about Jesus.

> *"When the Comforter is come, whom I will send unto you from the Father, even the Spirit of truth, which proceedeth from the Father, he shall testify of me: And ye also shall bear witness, because ye have been with me from the beginning."* John 15:26–27 (KJV)

Copy these verses from your Bible.

____

____

____

Have you ever watched TV court stories? If so, you know that "testify" means to make a statement based on your personal knowledge or belief about the defendant. Under oath to tell the truth, you tell what you know about a person's activities and personality.

Jesus states that both the Holy Spirit and His disciples will be witnesses about His words and actions. The day of Pentecost was a team effort. The disciples testified about the crucifixion and resurrection of Jesus. The Holy Spirit convicted and persuaded. The people believed and were saved.

4. To guide into all truth.

> *"Howbeit when he, the Spirit of truth, is come, he will guide you into all truth: for he shall not speak of himself; but whatsoever he shall hear, that shall he speak: and he will show you things to come."* John 16:13 (KJV)

Copy this verse from your Bible.

____

____

____

____

Another example of how the Holy Spirit helps us to know the truth and speak is found in Luke 12:11–12 (NIV). When you are brought to trial, *"Do not worry about how you will defend yourselves or what you will say, for the Holy Spirit will teach you at that time what you should say."*

5. To glorify Jesus.

> *"He shall glorify me: for he shall receive of mine, and shall show it unto you. All things that the Father hath are mine: therefore said I, that he shall take of mine, and shall show it unto you."* John 16:14–15 (KJV)

Copy these verses from your Bible.

____

____

____

____

The purpose of the Holy Spirit is to honor, exalt, and magnify Jesus Christ. How will He do this?

He will glorify Jesus through His believers. It will be through every part of our lives: what we say, how we act, and with whom we are friends. Our actions and our lips will bring honor to our Lord and Savior:

An example of this is found in Acts 7:55–56 (NIV). When the Sanhedrin was stoning Stephen, he honored Jesus:

> *Stephen, full of the Holy Spirit, looked up to heaven and saw the glory of God, and Jesus standing at the right hand of God. "Look," he said, "I see heaven open and the Son of Man standing at the right hand of God."*

DISCUSSION

1. When have you needed the Holy Spirit to be your Comforter?
2. Like the Holy Spirit testifies to us and shows us the truth about Jesus, we are supposed to testify to others. Who will you tell about Jesus? Ask the Holy Spirit to help you know what to say.

APPLICATION

1. How can we glorify Jesus? One way is through music. If you like to sing or know how to play an instrument, you can glorify Jesus through your song. Another way you can glorify Jesus is through writing. Try writing a poem that speaks about the Holy Spirit and how He comforts you. What other ways can you think of to glorify Jesus? Take some time to worship Him in a special way today.

2. A Verse to Memorize. Copy the verse below on an index card. Underline or print important words (shown in bold print) in color to help you remember the verse. You may want to color-code this verse in your Bible as well.

__Praise__ be to the __God__ and Father of our Lord __Jesus__ Christ,
the __Father__ of __compassion__ and the God of all __comfort__,
who comforts us in all our __troubles__,
so that we can __comfort__ those in any __trouble__
with the comfort we ourselves __receive__ from God.

2 Corinthians 1:3–4 (NIV), emphasis added

PRAYER

Heavenly Father,
You are great and do amazing things.
You alone are holy.
No one in heaven or earth is like You.
Your ways are higher and holier than our ways.
Your thoughts are greater and deeper than our thoughts.
Thank You for sending the Holy Spirit
to be my comforter and guide.
I will learn to trust Him when I face difficulties.
In Jesus' name I pray. Amen.

6

The Holy Spirit Convicts of Sin

Memory Verse: "When he *[the Holy Spirit]* comes, he will prove the world to be in the wrong about sin…because people do not believe in me."

JOHN 16:8–9 (NIV)

DO YOU HAVE A CONSCIENCE?

Did you ever start to pick up a piece of candy in a store, or copy the answer from your friend's test? Something inside told you, "That's wrong." And you stopped.

That was your conscience. It's an inner voice or feeling that makes you aware of what's right and wrong. It's a group of rules in your heart. Perhaps they were planted there by parents, teachers, or local laws. Everyone everywhere is born with a conscience. The Bible says:

Whether you turn to the
right or to the left,
your ears will hear a voice
behind you, saying,
"This is the way; walk in it."

Isaiah 30:21 (NIV)

SOMEONE GREATER THAN CONSCIENCE

In the spiritual world, the Holy Spirit is greater than your conscience. The first job of the Holy Spirit is to bring a feeling of guilt to unbelievers. Then He points them to the way of salvation.

Jesus said, *"When he* [the Holy Spirit] *comes, he will prove the world to be in the wrong about sin."* John 16:8 (NIV)

UNDERSTANDING WORDS

Two words that are important to know are conviction and repentance.

- *Conviction* is when the Holy Spirit helps a person who has sinned to know that what he or she did was wrong.
- *Repentance* is when a person is sincerely sorry for his or her actions.

In the life of a believer, these two words go hand in hand. When the Holy Spirit shows us that we have sinned, our response should be to pray and tell Jesus how sorry we are. Though we may face some hard consequences for our sinful choices, Jesus forgives us and helps us get back on the right track.

Do you remember Nicodemus?

Nicodemus was a Pharisee who asked Jesus about being born again.

Jesus replied, *"Very truly I tell you, no one can enter the kingdom of God unless they are born of water and the Spirit.... You must be born again."* John 3:5, 7 (NIV)

"Born again? How can this be?" Nicodemus was shocked!

Jesus explained that *born again* refers to spiritual rebirth. The Holy Spirit helps sinners see the truth of the gospel. He reveals their need to repent of their sins and accept Jesus Christ as their Savior.

Whoever responds positively to this pleading of the Holy Spirit—confessing sins and accepting Jesus as the Son of God—receives forgiveness and becomes a part of God's family.

All About Being Born Again

Read the conversation between Nicodemus and Jesus in John 3:1–9. Then find these words from the Bible in the puzzle below and circle them.

Again	**Enter**	**Kingdom**	**Teacher**
Birth	**Flesh**	**Sound**	**Truth**
Blows	**Gives**	**Spirit**	**Unless**
Born	**God**	**Surprised**	**Water**

```
T W A T E R A J Y D M D Z T E U F L E S H L Q P M
V F H Q S C F R V K B M S U B T U L A L C B S Y K
D D Q D M A C H Q G P S O J B V E M O D G N I K D
K R O X F P F F J R F Z D L H O H I L C W G L M B
O G K X P H Q L S B V U M A I L L K O N M M O O L
H T B X S Z D P V I I E H Y Q R I B G H Q Q R A U
V N A R X U Y F S A L Q U G J H C X V T N N S F J
I Z B M T B B I R T H C O A S L U Q U N L E S S O
F E N T E R E E M T V B D A K Y G A I S Y B J Y T
R F T S F H H M W N R W B P J L U I X A V U P I W
D H I J M R U B D E L T A O M A Q Y J T V G W W K
M I W S A D I Z H H O V A Z S N T U V C I L N L B
V S H T F T J C Y B L Y I Q Y K Y S F Y D R M Z O
M H R R Q Z A Y T D W V V O L E B X Q B Z O I X M
C D E D M E E N O F U E G Q T J P N J M S P K P U
V P W J T B J D T E O V Y O Y K D E S I R P R U S
C S C I D Y A R Y B W B L C S A N F H G H I J E H
Y W N A G A I N Z W D J S V E U K N Q B B T W X C
B O L F P D P Q K U W Z X R V W D N U O S W U C G
U L V P E D C X D W V D D A I O C U C C H A X R X
P B B N R X J K D G P I W D G R H T P Y F X O H T
```

He [God] anointed us, set his seal of ownership on us,
and put his Spirit in our hearts
as a deposit, guaranteeing what is to come.

2 Corinthians 1:21–22 (NIV)

Answers on page 121

Jesus promised His earthly followers that they would one day receive a heavenly reward. Being a Christian is not always easy, but we know we have a wonderful future ahead that is much greater than any trouble we have now. The Bible gives us many comforting reminders that encourage us and give us hope when problems come our way.

CHALLENGE

Reward of Believing

Find the Scriptures listed below in your Bible. Then write the Alphabet Letter in the box in front of the correct verse in the chart. The verses in the chart are from the NIV Bible. (Words may not be exactly the same in your translation, but you will recognize the verse.)

A. John 3:16
B. John 3:36
C. John 5:24
D. Romans 6:23
E. Galatians 6:7b–8
F. 1 John 5:13
G. Titus 3:5b–7
H. 1 Timothy 6:12

	"Whoever believes in the Son has eternal life, but whoever rejects the Son will not see life, for God's wrath remains on them."
	"For the wages of sin is death, but the gift of God is eternal life in Christ Jesus our Lord."
	"He saved us through the washing of rebirth and renewal by the Holy Spirit, whom he poured out on us generously through Jesus Christ our Savior, so that, having been justified by his grace, we might become heirs having the hope of eternal life."
	"For God so loved the world that he gave his one and only Son, that whoever believes in him shall not perish but have eternal life."
	"A man reaps what he sows. Whoever sows to please their flesh…will reap destruction; whoever sows to please the Spirit, from the Spirit will reap eternal life."
	"Fight the good fight of the faith. Take hold of the eternal life to which you were called when you made your good confession."
	"Very truly I tell you, whoever hears my word and believes him who sent me has eternal life and will not be judged but has crossed over from death to life."
	"I write these things to you who believe in the name of the Son of God so that you may know that you have eternal life."

Answers on page 121

DISCUSSION

1. How would you explain this statement? The Holy Spirit is to the Christian what the lighthouse is to the sailor.
2. Think or talk about these truths:
   a. Conviction points out our wrong doings, our sins.
   b. Repentance confesses our sins and stops them.

APPLICATION

1. Sing this chorus from "A Child of the King" by Harriet E. Buell.

   I'm a child of the King,
   A child of the King:
   With Jesus my Savior,
   I'm a child of the King!

2. A Verse to Memorize. Copy the verse below on an index card. Underline or print important words (shown in bold print) in color to help you remember the verse. You may want to color-code this verse in your Bible as well.

Very truly I tell you, ***whoever*** *hears my* ***word***
and ***believes*** *him who sent me has* ***eternal*** *life*
and will not be ***judged*** *but has* ***crossed*** *over from death to* ***life****.*

John 5:24 (NIV), emphasis added

PRAYER

Heavenly Father,
Blessed and holy is Your name.
Thank You for giving the Holy Spirit to me.
I'm so glad that He will continually help me choose between what is right and wrong.
I want to live an honest, helpful life for Jesus.
Help me to be a witness to my friends so that they may also know the peace the Holy Spirit gives.
I am grateful for His presence in my life.
I pray all this in the name of Jesus Christ. Amen.

7

The Holy Spirit Leads

Memory Verse: For those who are led by the Spirit of God are the children of God.

ROMANS 8:14 (NIV)

DEPENDABLE LEADERS

What makes someone a dependable leader? This leader is trustworthy. When this person says something, you can believe the words are true. A dependable leader's words and actions match. This person has proven to be steady and reliable.

Sometimes a dependable leader can be a thing instead of a person. Here are some examples of dependable leaders. What do they have in common?

1. The **North Star** led the Polynesian explorers to discover the Hawaiian Islands. It always remains stationary in the sky throughout the night.
2. The **compass** led Christopher Columbus through stormy seas to the Americas. The compass always points truly to the North.
3. God has given us the **Holy Spirit** to lead us on our life's journeys. This Spiritual Guide always points us in the right direction.

The Holy Spirit is a Christian's dependable leader. He shows us where to go. He also shows us where NOT to go. The more we read the Bible and pray, the more we come to understand the leading of the Holy Spirit. Sometimes we may ignore the message we receive from the Holy Spirit, either because we don't understand it, or we just don't want to obey. The choice we make can bring a lot of trouble our way that we might not have had if we had listened and obeyed Him right away.

MEET PHILIP, THE PREACHER

In the Bible, we read about the life of Philip. Not only was he a dependable leader for the new believers, he was also a faithful follower of the Holy Spirit.

The first time we meet Philip is in Acts 6:1–6. He was chosen by the apostles as one of seven men to care for the poor and the widows. These men had to be full of faith, wisdom, and the Holy Spirit.

Next, in Acts 8:5–8 we learn about Philip preaching the gospel in Samaria. He worked miracles and won many people to Christ.

READ A STORY

In Acts 8:26–39, you will see that the Holy Spirit chose Philip for an important task. What happened when Philip obeyed? Read this story to find out!

The Spirit Speaks and Acts

While Philip was preaching in Samaria, an angel of the Lord spoke to him. "Go south to the desert road that leads from Jerusalem down to Gaza," he said.

Philip did not question this strange message. He started out on foot immediately. Soon he saw a chariot moving slowly along the road.

The Spirit told Philip, "Go to that chariot and walk beside it."

In this chariot was a diplomat from Ethiopia. He was an important official in charge of all the treasury of the queen. He had gone to Jerusalem to worship. Now he was returning home.

As Philip neared the chariot, he heard the man reading from the scroll of Isaiah 53:7–8:

He was oppressed and afflicted,
yet he did not open his mouth;
he was led like a lamb to the slaughter,
and as a sheep before its shearers is silent,
so he did not open his mouth.
By oppression and judgment
he was taken away. (NIV)

Philip asked him, "Do you understand what you are reading?"

"How can I?" the man answered. "I have no one to explain these Scriptures to me."

He invited Philip to join him in his chariot.

First, Philip explained that the passage was about Jesus, the Suffering Servant. Then he told the official the good news about Jesus.

As they traveled along the road, they came to a body of water.

The man asked, "Is there any reason why I cannot be baptized and become a disciple of Jesus?"

"You can," Philip answered, "if you truly believe that Jesus Christ is the Son of God."

The official said, "I believe with all my heart."

The chariot stopped. Both Philip and the man went down into the water. Philip baptized him.

As they were coming up out of the water, the Spirit of the Lord carried Philip away. He was seen there no more. The Ethiopian went on his way rejoicing.

CHALLENGE

Doors Open; Doors Close

Let's learn more about how the Holy Spirit worked in the lives of some other faithful followers of Jesus. Print the correct letter above each symbol to read these messages from the Holy Spirit. For help, read Acts 13:1–4; Acts 16:6–8; Acts 22:17–18; Acts 23:11.

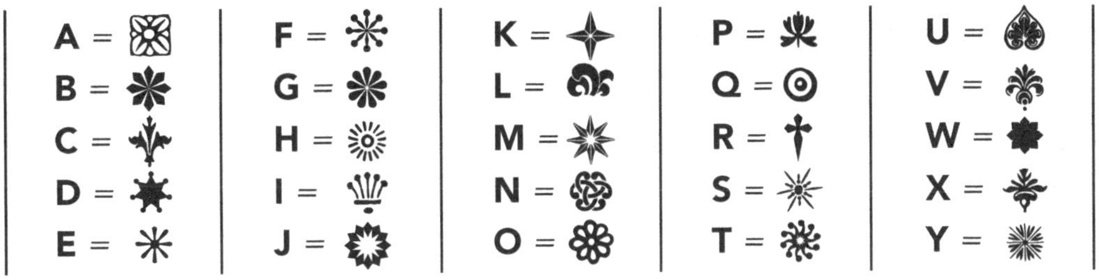

1. "Set apart for me —

___ ___ ___ ___ ___ ___ ___ ___ and ___ ___ ___ ___."

2. Two of them, sent...by the Holy Spirit, went down to —

___ ___ ___ ___ ___ ___ ___ and ___ ___ ___ ___ ___ ___.

3. The Holy Spirit would not let them preach in the —

___ ___ ___ ___ ___ ___ ___ ___ of ___ ___ ___ ___.

4. They tried to enter Bithynia but the Spirit —

___ ___ ___ ___ ___ not ___ ___ ___ ___ ___ ___ ___.

5. Paul fell into a trance, and the Lord said —

"___ ___ ___ ___ ___ ___ ___ ___ ___ ___ ___ ___ ___ ___."

6. The Lord stood near Paul and said —

"___ ___ ___ ___ ___ ___ ___ ___ ___ ___ ___."

Answers on page 121

From what we have just learned, we can see how the Holy Spirit led Christians long ago. But does He still lead us today? How does He do that? We can find the answer to those questions in the Bible!

How Believers Received Messages from God

The writers of the New Testament used different titles to represent the Trinity (God, Jesus, and the Holy Spirit) as they spoke to or led believers. Read the Scripture in **Column 1** to find out how the person in **Column 2** received a message in **Column 3**. Fill in the answers.

1. Scripture	2. Person(s)	3. How was the message sent?
Luke 1:26–28		
Matthew 2:12		
Matthew 2:19		
Luke 4:1		
Acts 8:39		
Acts 9:10		
Acts 10:3		
Acts 10:13		
Acts 13:1–2		
Acts 22:17–18		

Answers on page 122

DISCUSSION

1. Have you ever made plans to go someplace, but something blocked the way, like it did with Saul (later known as Paul)?
2. Think or talk about the Holy Spirit's ability:
    a) To see the future
    b) To protect from danger and problems
    c) To lead our lives

APPLICATION

1. When you make plans, be sure to say, "Your will be done!" or "If God is willing." Why? Read James 4:13–15 to find out.
2. A Verse to Memorize. Copy the verse below on an index card. Underline or print important words (shown in bold print) in color to help you remember the verse. You may want to color-code this verse in your Bible as well.

Trust** in the **LORD** with all your **heart
*and **lean** not on your own **understanding**;*
*in all your ways **submit** to him,*
*and he will **make** your paths **straight**.*

Proverbs 3:5–6 (NIV), emphasis added

PRAYER

Heavenly Father,
You are holy and full of love for all Your creation.
Thank You for sending Your Spirit to guide my steps.
I will trust You to show me the way.
I will try to be aware when You open doors and close doors.
I will not complain when You change my plans.
I want to be like Phillip and Paul who followed your directions without questions or complaints.
Please help me be a blessing to my family and friends.
In the precious name of Jesus, I pray. Amen.

8

The Holy Spirit Gives Joy

Memory Verse: At that time Jesus, full of joy through the Holy Spirit, said, "I praise you, Father, Lord of heaven and earth, because you have hidden these things from the wise and learned, and revealed them to little children. Yes, Father, for this is what you were pleased to do."

LUKE 10:21 (NIV)

WHAT IS JOY?

Did you ever sing that song that gives the definition of "JOY"?
"**J**esus first. **Y**ourself last. And **O**thers in between."

What is the difference between happiness and joy? Happiness is based on events, environment, or relationships. True joy rises above circumstances and focuses on our spiritual walk with God. It is present even in times of sorrow or loss. Joy is a God-given emotion—a spiritual gift of the Holy Spirit.

In this chapter we will search for people who experienced that gift of joy or verses that describe what it is.

A BABY LEAPS FOR JOY!

After Mary learned that she was pregnant with the Son of God, she went to visit her cousin Elizabeth in the hill country of Judea. Through a miracle, Elizabeth was pregnant with a baby boy who would become John the Baptist.

Read Luke 1:39–45 (NIV) to fill in the missing letters.

Verse 41. When ___ ___ ___ Z ___ ___ ___ ___ ___ heard Mary's

___ ___ ___ ___ ___ ___ ___ G, the baby ___ ___ ___ P ___ ___ in her womb, and

Elizabeth was ___ I ___ ___ ___ ___ with the ___ ___ L ___ S ___ ___ ___ ___ ___.

Verse 42. In a loud voice, Elizabeth said, "___ ___ ___ S ___ ___ ___ are you among ___ ___ M ___ ___ , and blessed is the ___ ___ ___ ___ D you will ___ ___ A ___!"

Verse 44. Elizabeth continued, "As soon as the ___ O ___ ___ ___ of your greeting ___ ___ ___ C ___ ___ ___ my ears, the ___ ___ B ___ in my W___ ___ ___ leaped for ___ O ___."

Verse 45. "Blessed is she who has ___ ___ ___ ___ ___ V ___ ___ that the ___ ___ R ___ would fulfill his ___ ___ ___ M ___ ___ ___ ___ to her!"

THE JOY WE HAVE

The Bible has a lot to say about joy. As Christians, we have the Source of joy living inside us. Our actions and our words, as well as our faces, should show others how wonderful it is to live for Jesus and to have the Holy Spirit to help us every day. When our friends see that joy in us, they will want it too!

Eight Words in the Joy Family

Blessed	**Delight**	**Happy**	**Pleasing**
Cheerful	**Glad**	**Joy**	**Rejoice**

Read the following verses about joy in your NIV Bible and fill in all blanks. Highlight any of the above words from the Joy Family.

1. Psalm 9:1–2. "I will give ____________ to you, LORD, with all my ______________; I will tell of all your wonderful ___________. I will be _________ and ______________ in you; I will ___________ the ________________ of your name, O Most High."

2. Psalm 112:1. "______________are those who ________the LORD, who find great ______________ in his _________________."

3. Matthew 5:11–12. "______________ are you when people insult you, __________________ you and falsely _______ all kinds of __________ against you because of me. ______________ and be ________, because great is your _____________ in _____________."

4. Luke 10:20b. "But ____________ that _______ ____________ are written in

__________________."

5. John 16:24. "Until now you have not asked for anything in my name. Ask and you will

_______________, and your _________ will be __________________."

6. Romans 14:17–18. "For the kingdom of God is...righteousness, __________ and

_______ in the _________ __________, because anyone who __________Christ in

this way is ____________to God."

7. Philippians 4:4. "______________ in the __________ always. I will say it again:

______________!"

8. 1 Peter 1:8. "Though you have not _________ him, you _________ him; and even

though you do not see him now, you ______________ in him and are ______________

with an inexpressible and glorious ________."

Find Memorable Truths

Unscramble the letters below the lines to complete the Bible verses. Look up the Scripture references to check your answers.

1. The ___ ___ ___ of the ___ ___ ___ ___ is ___ ___ ___ ___
O Y J / D L O R / U R O Y

___ ___ ___ ___ ___ ___ ___ ___ ___.
T H T E R G S N

2. A ___ ___ ___ ___ ___ ___ ___ ___ ___ ___ ___ ___ ___ is
F L E R C H U E / T H A R E

___ ___ ___ ___ ___ ___ ___ ___ ___ ___ ___ ___ ___.
O D G O / D I C E N I M E

3. A ___ ___ ___ ___ ___ ___ ___ ___ ___ ___ ___ ___ ___ ___ ___
P H Y A P / H A T E R / A S K M E

the ___ ___ ___ ___ ___ ___ ___ ___ ___ ___ ___ ___ ___.
C A F E / C L U E F E H R

Helpful Hints in NIV: 1. Nehemiah 8:10b. 2. Proverbs 17:22a. 3. Proverbs 15:13a.

Answers on page 122

CHALLENGE

Conversion of the Jailer

Read Acts 16:22–34

Paul and Silas were traveling as missionaries, telling everyone about Jesus. Now they were in a terrible situation. They had every reason to be sad and angry. Instead, they praised God, and something amazing happened!

Use the clues to solve the crossword puzzle. Read the Bible verses above if you need help.

Across

3. Paul shouted, "Don't ___ yourself!"

4. The jailer fell ___ before Paul and Silas.

7. The jailer and his household were ___.

8. Suddenly there was a violent ___.

10. At midnight, Paul and Silas were ___.

13. What flew open?

14. Who ordered Paul and Silas to be beaten?

16. Paul and Silas were thrown into ___.

17. What did the jailer do to their wounds?

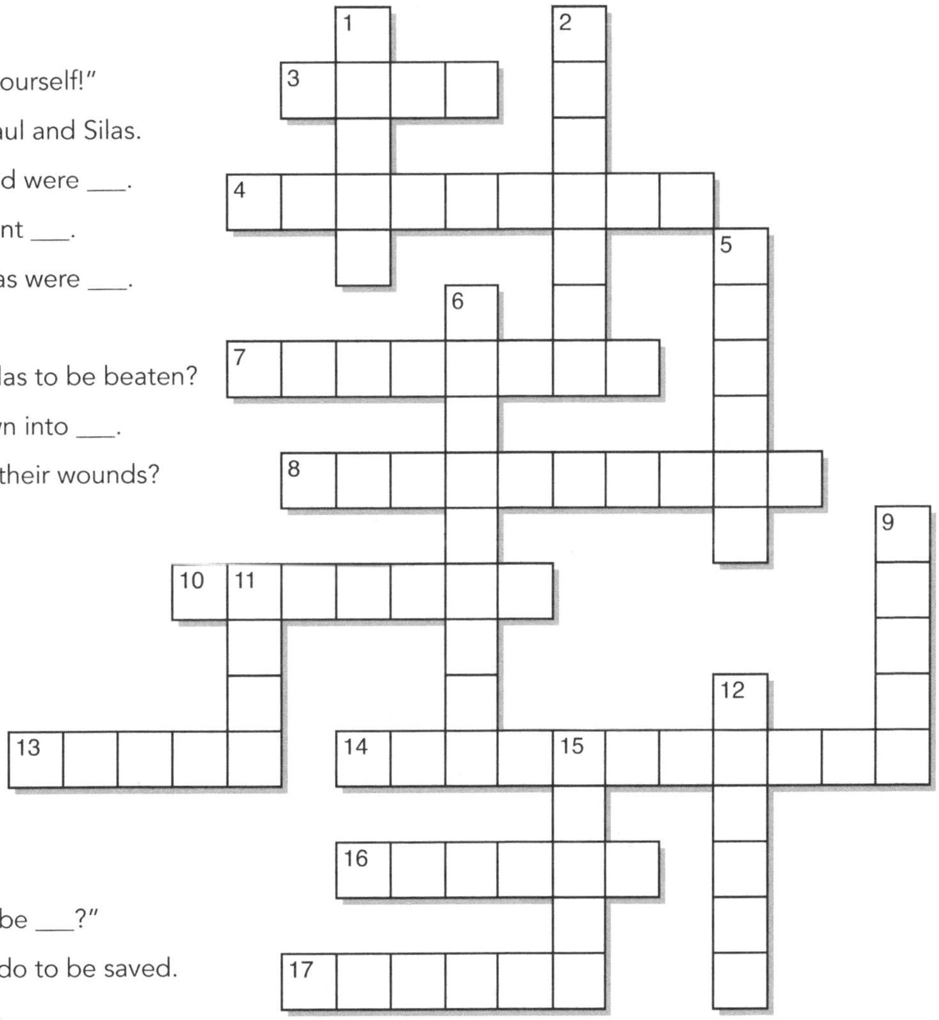

Down

1. Jailer: "What must I do to be ___?"

2. What the jailer needed to do to be saved.

5. Their feet were fastened in ___.

6. What were the prisoners doing?

9. Paul and Silas were singing ___.

11. They were beaten with ___.

12. Who would be guarding them?

15. Jailer drew his ___ to kill himself.

The jailer brought them into his house and set a meal before them; he was filled with joy because he had come to believe in God—he and his whole household.

Acts 16:34 (NIV)

Answers on page 122

DISCUSSION

1. Review Acts 16:22–34. When and in how many ways did the Holy Spirit work in this story?
2. In how many ways did Paul and Silas live out their Christian faith? What do you think would have happened if the men had been silent in jail instead?

APPLICATION

1. Walking with God brings great joy. To walk like this, you need a pair of strong, balanced legs: Prayer and Praise. Draw a picture or cartoon of a person, making one leg "prayer" and the other "praise."
2. A Verse to Memorize. Copy the verse below on an index card. Underline or print important words (shown in bold print) in color to help you remember the verse. You may want to color-code this verse in your Bible as well.

__Blessed__ is the one…
whose __delight__ is in the __law__ of the __LORD__,
and who __meditates__ on his law __day__ and __night__.

Psalm 1:1–2 (NIV), emphasis added

PRAYER

Heavenly Father,
You are rich in love and slow to anger.
You are a plentiful provider of all good things.
I praise You for Your mighty deeds.
I praise You because You are the only true God,
a living God, a miracle-working God.
I need to be more aware of Your good blessings in my life
and express thanksgiving for them.
Thank You for Your wonderful gifts of joy and peace.
Help me remember that joy is a gift of the Holy Spirit
and show me how to share it with others.
I ask all this in the name of Jesus. Amen.

9

The Holy Spirit Empowers

Memory Verse: I pray that out of his glorious riches he may strengthen you with power through his Spirit in your inner being, so that Christ may dwell in your hearts through faith.

EPHESIANS 3:16–17 (NIV)

The Holy Spirit empowers those who follow Jesus. He gives us strength and the ability to serve Him in ways we could not do on our own. With the Holy Spirit's help, we can reach people in our own hometown or around the world with the good news about Jesus!

READ A STORY

Would you like to become a storyteller? After you fill in the blanks, you will be ready to tell the story of Dorcas found in Acts 9:36–42. If you like, three readers may present the story, or you may read all the parts yourself.

A Marvelous Miracle in Joppa

READERS: **Speaker One**—starts telling the story, adding background information found in research

Speaker Two—continues telling the background information

Speaker Three—reads the Bible verses

One: A Christian woman, dedicated to doing good works, lived in Joppa—a seaport city on the Mediterranean Sea.

Three: (Verse 36) This disciple was named Tabitha. Her Greek name was________________. She was always helping the ____________.

One: Dorcas was a generous person. She gave her life, time, and talents in service to widows. She was a gifted seamstress.

Two: She purchased fabric with her own money. Then she cut out articles of clothing without patterns. Although she had no sewing machine, she sewed garments with needle and thread for the widows and their children.

One: Dorcas was empowered to do and give, to serve and share.

Three: (Verse 37) One day she became very ________ and ________. Her ________ was ______________ and ______________ in an ________________ room, awaiting burial.

One: The apostle Peter was ministering in Lydda, a town about 17 miles from Joppa.

Two: Two disciples hurried to Lydda. They asked Peter to come at once to Joppa because Dorcas, a Christian, had just died.

Three: (Verse 39) Peter ________ with them. When he arrived, he was taken ______________ to the room. All the ____________ stood around him ____________. They ______________ him the ___________ and other ______________ that _____________ had made for them.

Two: Peter sent everyone out of the room. Then he knelt on his knees beside her bed and began to pray.

One: Perhaps the Holy Spirit reminded Peter what Jesus had told His disciples. They would do even greater miracles than He had done. With faith in this promise, Peter prayed the Holy Spirit would empower him to perform an amazing miracle.

Two: Turning toward the dead woman, he said, "Tabitha, get up." She opened her eyes. When she saw Peter, she sat up.

Three: (Verse 41) Peter took Dorcas by the ________ and _____________ her to her _________. Then he called for the ____________________, especially the _____________, and he __________________ her to them _____________.

One: This was a moment of great rejoicing. Widows who had been weeping were now praising God for His goodness to them.

Three: (Verse 42) Soon the news spread throughout __________. Apostle Peter had raised Dorcas from the dead through the ____________ of the Holy Spirit. As a result, many people ______________ in the __________ and were saved.

—The End—

A PROMISE AND AN ASSIGNMENT

Read the Bible verses to fill in the blanks.

Just before Jesus ascended into heaven, He gave a final promise to His disciples, recorded in Acts 1:8 (NIV). *"You will receive* ___________ *when the* _________ ____________ *comes on you; and you will be my* _______________ *in Jerusalem, and in all Judea and Samaria, and to the* _________ *of the* _____________*."*

That promise is for us too. Christians today will be empowered to witness to people in our part of the "ends of the earth."

Empowerment Means Doing—Serving

Each of us is given a special task to do. We receive enough power from the Holy Spirit to do it well.

How do we see evidence of this in ourselves and others?

1. By telling others about Jesus Christ.

Fill in the blanks using an NIV Bible.

The primary purpose of empowerment is to witness about Jesus. He said, *"Whoever* ______________________ *me before others, I will also* ____________________ *before my* __________ *in heaven."* (Matthew 10:32 NIV)

"You are my _______________*," declares the* L*ORD, "and my* _______________ *whom I have chosen."* (Isaiah 43:10 NIV)

2. Through our character shown in the life we live.

An old proverb says: Actions speak louder than words.

Accomplishment depends more on what we *are* than on what we *know*. George Washington and Abraham Lincoln were both elected to the presidency of the United States because of character, not knowledge.

3. By the forgiveness we offer.

During World War II, Corrie ten Boom and her family hid hundreds of Jews in a secret closet to protect them from Nazi authorities. A fellow Dutch citizen betrayed them. Corrie's entire family was imprisoned in February 1944.

Corrie and her sister, Betsie, were held in three different prisons for the next ten months. The last one was the Ravensbrück concentration camp near Berlin in Germany. Here they both endured horrible treatment. Betsie died in prison. Corrie was finally released in December of 1944.

After her pardon, Corrie began preaching about forgiveness. In 1947 she faced a test in Munich at one of her meetings. After the service, a man came up and wanted to shake her hand. Corrie instantly recognized him as one of the cruelest guards at Ravensbrück. How could she shake his hand?

This former guard told her he had become a Christian. He believed God had forgiven him. Now he needed to hear from Corrie. Would she forgive him for the evil he had done?

In Christian love, Corrie shook his hand and forgave him.

Later, she told her story in a book entitled *The Hiding Place.*

4. By the compassion we offer to the needy.

What is the difference between pity and compassion? "Pity weeps and walks away. Compassion comes to help and stay."

An excellent example of compassion is found in the life of Mother Teresa. She was a Catholic nun who devoted her life to serving the poor and destitute around the world. She spent many years in Calcutta, India.

She made it her mission to look after neglected people. Mother Teresa felt that serving others was a fundamental principle of the teachings of Jesus Christ. She often repeated something Jesus said, "Whatever you do to the least of my brethren, you do it to me."

In 1952, she opened her first home for the dying, which allowed people to die with dignity. Mother Teresa gave loving care to the neglected along with the opportunity to die knowing that someone cared.

> *"Not all of us can do great things.*
> *But we can do small things with great love."*
>
> Mother Teresa

CHALLENGE

Empowerment is a gift of the Holy Spirit. But to develop that gift, you need to follow Paul's formula for defeating sin and the devil.

Find the right words in Ephesians 6:10–18 to complete this acrostic and to be *"strong in the Lord and in his mighty power."*

Put on the Full Armor of God

F ___ ___ ___ ___

___ ___ **U** ___ ___

___ ___ **L** ___

___ ___ **L** ___ ___ ___ ___ ___ ___

___ ___ ___ **A** ___ ___ ___ ___ ___ ___ ___

___ ___ ___ **R** ___ ___

___ ___ ___ **M** ___ ___

___ ___ ___ ___ ___ ___ **O** ___ ___ ___ ___ ___ ___

___ **R** ___ ___ ___ ___ ___

___ **O** ___ ___

F ___ ___ ___

G ___ ___ ___ ___ ___

___ ___ **O** ___ ___

___ ___ ___ ___ ___ **D**

Answers on page 122

DISCUSSION

1. What do you think this quotation means?
   "Character is the diamond that scratches every other stone."
   Character is more important than ________________ done or______________ spoken.
2. Thinking of Dorcas, do you have a talent you can use for Jesus?
   If you aren't sure, how can you discover your talent?
   a. Think about what you do that other people compliment.
   b. Think about what you have done that makes you feel glad.

APPLICATION

1. Draw a picture of a soldier clothed in the full armor of God.
2. A Verse to Memorize. Copy the verse below on an index card. Underline or print important words (shown in bold print) in color to help you remember the verse. You may want to color-code this verse in your Bible as well.

*I **can** do **all** things through **Christ** who **strengthens** me.*

Philippians 4:13 (NKJV), emphasis added

PRAYER

Use Scripture verses to express your praise (ex. Psalm 145:8–9) or for making requests (ex. Hebrews 13:20–21).

Heavenly Father,
You are gracious and compassionate,
slow to anger and rich in love.
You are good to all and
You have compassion on all You have made.
Thank You for directing my steps.
Thank You for the blessings (name some) *that You have given*
my family.
Now, God of power and peace, please equip and empower me
with everything I need for doing Your will.
Please work in me in whatever way is pleasing to You.
In the precious name of Jesus, I ask all this. Amen.

10

The Holy Spirit Gives Wisdom

Memory Verse: I keep asking that the God of our Lord Jesus Christ, the glorious Father, may give you the Spirit of wisdom and revelation, so that you may know him better.

EPHESIANS 1:17 (NIV)

WHAT IS WISDOM?

Name someone you know who is wise. ______________________________

Is that person old or young? Does he read lots of books? Did she go to school for a long time? How do people become wise?

The dictionary states that wisdom is made up of experience, knowledge, and good judgment. The Bible has much more to tell us about wisdom. Let's see what God's Word teaches us about this important subject and how the Holy Spirit gives us wisdom.

The Value of Wisdom

Solomon, the wisest man who ever lived, wrote about wisdom in Proverbs 3:13–17. Use an NIV Bible to fill in the blanks to learn about "her."

Verse 13. *"Blessed are those who find ______________, those who gain ________________________,*

Verse 14. *for she is more __________________ than ____________ and yields better _______________ than __________.*

Verse 15. *She is more ________________ than ______________; nothing you ______________ can _________________ with her.*

Verse 16. *Long _________ is in her ___________ hand; in her __________ hand are ____________ and _____________.*

Verse 17. *Her ways are _______________ ways, and all her ___________ are peace."*

An Example of Wisdom

Read Isaiah 11:1–3 (NIV) to learn an Old Testament prophecy that describes the wisdom of Jesus. Then fill in the blanks.

> *"A shoot will come up from the stump of Jesse;*
> *from his roots a Branch will bear fruit.*
>
> *The Spirit of the LORD will rest on him—*
>
> *the Spirit of ____________ and of ________________________,*
>
> *the Spirit of ________________ and of _______________,*
>
> *the Spirit of the ____________________ and __________ of the LORD —*
>
> *and he will _______________ in the _________ of the LORD."*
>
> (To *fear* God is to respond to Him in awe, trust, obedience, and worship.[1])

The Source of Wisdom

As you read, study, and learn throughout your life, you will gain much knowledge. Nothing compares to the special kind of wisdom we receive from God.

> *"The LORD gives _____________; from his mouth come _________________*
>
> *and ______________________."* Proverbs 2:6 (NIV)

Note: LORD in all capital letters means God. Lord means Jesus Christ.

THE HOLY SPIRIT IN THE OLD TESTAMENT

Although the Holy Spirit was first sent to people at Pentecost, He also is found at work in Old Testament times. God often sent help to a special person for a special event. Here are two examples:

1. Read Exodus 35:30–35 and complete the sentence. God chose Bezalel and filled him with ____

   ____ .

2. After Jerusalem was destroyed, the people were taken captive. Daniel and his three teenage friends were forced to go to Babylon to live, but God was with them.

1. Walvoord, John, and Roy Zuck. *The Bible Knowledge Commentary / Old, Old Testament.* Wheaton, Ill., Victor Books, 1989.

READ A PLAY

This play is based on Daniel 2:1–49. Let's learn more about how the Holy Spirit was with Daniel and gave him wisdom far beyond what any other man of that time had.

God Gives Daniel Wisdom

CAST:
- **Narrator**—storyteller who explains background and action
- **King Nebuchadnezzar**—king of Babylon
- **Wise Man 1**—a magician
- **Wise Man 2**—a fortune teller
- **Arioch**—commander of the king's guard
- **Daniel**—captive teenager from Jerusalem

Scene—In the king's courtyard and at Daniel's home

Narrator: King Nebuchadnezzar had a weird dream. His mind was so troubled that he could not sleep. He called in his wise men and told them his dream.

King: I have had a dream that troubles me. I want to know what it means.

Wise Man 1: May the king live forever! Tell your servants the dream, and we will interpret it.

King: First, you must tell me my dream. Then I want you to explain it.

Wise Man 2: Let the king tell us his dream. Then we will explain it.

King: If you do not tell me my dream and what it means, I will have you cut into pieces. I will destroy your houses. But if you tell me my dream and explain it, you will receive rewards and great honor.

Wise Man 1: There is no one on earth who can do what you ask!

King: You are just trying to gain time. I believe you have plotted to tell me false and evil things, hoping the situation will change. I have firmly decided what I will do. Tell me the dream and explain it or else!

Wise Man 2: No king has ever asked such a thing of any wise man.

Wise Man 1: No one can reveal it to you, O King, except the gods, and they do not live among humans.

Narrator:	The king was so angry that he ordered the execution of all wise men of Babylon. The decree was issued to put all wise men to death. Soldiers were sent to look for Daniel and his friends. Arioch, the commander of the king's guard, found Daniel.
Arioch:	The king has issued a decree that all wise men are to be put to death. That includes you, Daniel.
Daniel:	Why did the king issue such a harsh decree?
Narrator:	After Arioch explained the matter, Daniel went in to talk to the king.
Daniel:	O King, please give us more time so that I can interpret the dream for you.
Narrator:	Daniel went home and talked with his three friends and asked them to pray. They all begged for mercy from God concerning this request. During the night, the mystery was revealed to Daniel in a vision. And he honored God.
Daniel:	Praise be to the name of God for ever and ever. Wisdom and power are His. He gives wisdom to the wise and knowledge to the discerning. Holy God, You have given me wisdom and power. You have made known to me what we asked of You. You have made known to me the dream of the king.
Narrator:	Daniel went to Arioch.
Daniel:	Do not execute the wise men of Babylon. Take me to King Nebuchadnezzar, and I will interpret his dream.
Narrator:	Arioch took Daniel to the king.
King:	Are you able to tell me what I saw in my dream and what it means?
Daniel:	No wise man or magician can explain your dream. But there is a God in heaven who reveals mysteries. He has shown you, O King, what will happen in days to come.
Narrator:	Then Daniel told the king his dream and the meaning of it. The king fell face down before Daniel in awe, wonder, and praise.
King:	Surely your God is the God of gods and the Lord of kings, and a revealer of mysteries.

Narrator: The decree was cancelled. No wise men were killed. Instead, Daniel and his three friends were given rewards and places of high honor in the kingdom.

—The End—

"The ________ of the L*ORD is the beginning of __________________."*
Proverbs 1:7 (NIV)

CHALLENGE

Gifts from God

God gives gifts to special people. Some of these gifts are hidden in this jungle of letters. To find them, color every square that has a Q, X, or Z with colors of your choice. Then read the message in the uncolored squares. Finally, fill in the blanks below.

Q	X	T	O	Z	Q	X	Z	T	H	E	Q	X
Z	Q	Z	P	E	R	S	O	N	Z	Q	X	Z
W	H	O	Z	X	Q	Z	X	Q	Q	X	Z	Q
X	Q	X	Q	Z	X	P	L	E	A	S	E	S
Q	Z	Z	H	I	M	Q	Z	X	Z	Q	X	Z
Z	G	O	D	Q	Z	X	G	I	V	E	S	X
X	Q	W	I	S	D	O	M	Z	Q	Z	Q	Z
Q	Z	X	Q	K	N	O	W	L	E	D	G	E
Z	A	N	D	Q	Z	X	Q	X	Z	Q	Z	X
X	Q	H	A	P	P	I	N	E	S	S	X	Q
E	C	C	L	E	S	I	A	S	T	E	S	Z
X	Z	C	H	A	P	T	E	R	X	2	Q	X
Z	Q	X	Z	V	E	R	S	E	Z	2	6	Q

To the person who ____________________ God, He gives three gifts:

1.______________, 2.______________________, 3. ________________.

Where is this verse found in the Old Testament? (*Color it purple.*) ____________________

Answers on page 122

DISCUSSION

1. Note the three words that often come together in the Bible: Wisdom, Understanding, Knowledge. How are these words related to each other?
2. What did Daniel do to get wisdom?
3. "Knowing what is right and doing it." Why is this a good definition of wisdom?

APPLICATION

1. Here's a bit of wisdom you can copy and post on your mirror.

   "Character cannot be developed in ease and quiet. Only through experience of trial and suffering can the soul be strengthened, vision cleared, ambition inspired, and success achieved." Helen Keller

2. A Verse to Memorize. Copy the verse below on an index card. Underline or print important words (shown in bold print) in color to help you remember the verse. You may want to color-code this verse in your Bible as well.

If any of you ***lacks wisdom****,*
you should ***ask*** *God, who gives* ***generously***
to all without ***finding*** *fault, and it will be* ***given*** *to* ***you****.*
But when you ask, you must ***believe*** *and not* ***doubt****.*

James 1:5–6 (NIV), emphasis added

PRAYER

Write a prayer, telling God how wise He is. Use phrases from Psalm 86.

Thank God for when He has helped you in times of trouble or confusion.
Talk to Him about the needs of your family.
Ask Him for wisdom and strength, so you can make the best decisions.
Close in the name of Jesus, the Son of God.

11

The Holy Spirit Encourages

Memory Verse: Then the church throughout Judea, Galilee and Samaria enjoyed a time of peace and was strengthened. Living in the fear of the Lord and encouraged by the Holy Spirit, it increased in numbers.

ACTS 9:31 (NIV)

God gives each person some jobs to do. Think about the people in your family. Your parents probably have a job outside of the home so they can earn money to provide what your family needs. They also have jobs inside the home, like mowing the lawn and cooking dinner.

What jobs do you have? Write some of them here.

____

____

When everyone in the family does their job, life at home is happier and things run a lot smoother!

DUTIES OF THE HOLY SPIRIT

You have already learned some of the important jobs the Holy Spirit does. He comforts, leads, empowers, and gives us wisdom. What else does He do?

Read the Bible verse. Then fill in the blanks.

John 14:15–17 (NIV). *"If you love me, keep my commands. And I will ask the Father, and he will give you another ________________ to help you and be with you ________________—the Spirit of truth."*

In the original version of the Holy Bible, the Greek word *parakletos* can mean advocate, comforter, counselor, encourager, or helper. All these titles then become true jobs of the Holy Spirit.

How Does the Holy Spirit Help Us?

The Bible explains what the Holy Spirit does in our lives. Read the list of jobs and descriptions. Then read the Bible verses and decide which ones match the descriptions. Draw the symbol from the "His Jobs" Column in the correct boxes in Columns 2 and 3.

His Jobs	Description of His Jobs	Scriptures
Educates 	The Holy Spirit floods our hearts with the love of God.	Romans 8:26–27
Jogs your Memory 	By the power of the Holy Spirit, the hope, joy, and peace of God will spill over in you.	John 14:26a
Prays and Pleads 	The Holy Spirit will teach you all things.	Romans 5:5
Fills with Love 	The Holy Spirit testifies with our spirit that we are the children of God.	Romans 15:13
Bears Witness 	The Spirit helps us in our weakness. He intercedes for God's people.	John 14:26b
Gives Hope, Joy, and Peace 	The Holy Spirit will remind you of everything Jesus has said.	Romans 8:16

As the Encouraging One

The Holy Spirit comes alongside us to give aid and help. Family and friends are not always available to support you when needed. But for Christians, the Holy Spirit is always present to encourage us…anytime and anywhere. He can do this because God's ______________ ______________ ____ ________ ______________. 1 Corinthians 3:16b (NIV)

What Encouragement Can Do

When we are encouraged by the Holy Spirit, we want to encourage others by sharing what God has done for us. When we tell others, we are giving our *testimony*—the true, personal story of what has happened to us. The Holy Spirit's encouragement doesn't have to stop with one person; it can spread on and on!

Answers on page 122

Read the Bible verses and fill in the blanks to see what happened when Barnabas spoke encouraging words to others.

Acts 11:23–24 (NIV). *"When he* [Barnabas] *arrived and saw what the grace of God had done, he was* __________ *and* ____________________ *them all to remain true to the Lord with all their hearts. He was a* ________ *man, full of the* __________ ______________ *and* _____________, *and a great number of* ________________ *were* _______________ *to the Lord."*

READ A STORY

Who Was Barnabas?

Joseph lived in Cyprus, a large island in the Mediterranean Sea. When he became a Christian, he sold his land and gave the money to the apostles in Jerusalem. (Acts 4:36)

This Christian leader gained the nickname of Barnabas (BAR-nuh-bus)—son of encouragement—because of the help he provided the apostles.

Early in church history, Barnabas traveled to Antioch to check on a group of new Christians. Then he journeyed to Tarsus. He brought Saul back to minister with him to the Christians in Antioch. Because of his good reputation, Barnabas was able to calm the people's fears about Saul. He persuaded the disciples in Jerusalem that Saul had become a true Christian. Barnabas recognized that Saul had great potential. He took him as a partner to help mold him to be a leader.

Barnabas did wonders with encouragement. He taught and trained Saul, later called Paul, and John Mark, his nephew. Barnabas was a strong, but silent leader in the church. His influence on these men can never be measured. Paul was the author of 13 epistles. John Mark was the author of the Gospel of Mark.

Later, Paul passed on this message:

"Therefore ________________ *one another and* _____________ ________ _________ _____, *just as in fact you are doing"* (1 Thessalonians 5:11 NIV).

Was Barnabas' effort effective?

Be a Barnabas!

How can you be like Barnabas? You can encourage others! In Hebrews 10:24–25 (NIV), the Bible says, *"Let us consider how we may spur one another on toward love and good deeds...encouraging one another."*

You never know how your words may help someone. Maybe the encouraging words you say today will even lead someone to become a follower of Jesus tomorrow!

CHALLENGE

How to Encourage Others

These verbs will help you become an encourager. Circle them in the puzzle below. Words may be hidden forwards, backwards, up, down, or horizontally.

Appreciate	Cheer	Honor	Persevere	Serve
Assist	Comfort	Inspire	Praise	Share
Boost	Compliment	Love	Pray	Stimulate
Build	Edify	Motivate	Reassure	Support
Carry	Help	Notice	Rejoice	Understand

I N S P I R E H R W X O S F N L B T Q U S U W R L
D F Y H B D F E T A I C E R P P A Z H F H F P F W
B M Q O U Z C U Q J D Z T K V C A E T A V I T O M
O H L E I A S U N W S X T T J R J E V M A H S U S
O K K J L F O Y S T O P F B P E H W X T T V N X K
S D I C D J G V I H H J C G N A X A Y U N A Z C X
T S M H D P A M X I A K Q F Y S Q A T U E O V A O
R E S E Q F U P H K Y R N P X S D H J D V R X B Z
U R O E Q L B K T Y U N U A C U S B A L I X A R A
U V H R A V I G Z W S X P H A R V T J H N F O H Z
T E L T Q H S Z P T X R W Y P E L Q L R C N B U S
T K E E O H E E M Q I Q W U Y Q C W S R O O E U I
H P V N E L V C I L U W C X N V J I G H O A C H Z
Q L A U O O B O X V C I G K B D L Y O H I K D O F
W U Q Y L P F Y K C T S H C K T E Y W J Z Y A R P
S C O M P L I M E N T P Z E A G Z R X D E C W F I
F U C A E R P K Y R I Y W C S B D H S B Y R V C S
C E I V J R G F E G Z O I I C H X X L T O V T T E
C K S I S B E G R S K T Z T J N I J V A A R L S U
E E I W U X C V C C R F T O Y J U H L C O N Y I Q
F S W Y H A H H E O Y H U N P R Y C U F J Z D S C
R I Q R K B U N P S R X C J O F Z F M W P D O S E
C A E A Q I K P K X R Z L F K O W O I H O M N A D
J R W Z X P U X D T A E Y U J O C U S D V V V T S
D P D S J S U R G U C Z P T C G W P D U E P L E H

Answers on page 122

DISCUSSION

1. Here are a few statements to think about. How can you use them?
   * "A word of encouragement during a failure is worth more than an hour of praise after success."
   * "Never get tired of doing little things for others. Sometimes those little things occupy the biggest part of their hearts."
   * "Be somebody who makes everybody feel like a somebody."

APPLICATION

1. Look for ways to truly praise parents, teachers, or coaches. People in authority seldom hear kind words.
2. Express thanks for things done for you.
3. A Verse to Memorize. Copy the verse below on an index card. Underline or print important words (shown in bold print) in color to help you remember the verse. You may want to color-code this verse in your Bible as well. (You might want to color this verse brown since it tells the duties and responsibilities of a Christian.)

Do not let any ***unwholesome*** *talk come* ***out*** *of your* ***mouths****,*
but ***only*** *what is* ***helpful***
for ***building*** *others up* ***according*** *to their* ***needs****.*

Ephesians 4:29 (NIV), emphasis added

PRAYER

Heavenly Father,
You are a great God, full of love and mercy.
Your love is steadfast and never ceases.
Your mercies are new every morning.
And I am a receiver of that love and forgiveness.
Thank You for protecting Your Holy Bible for centuries.
Now I am able to read about the Holy Spirit
and the disciples who carried on the work of Jesus.
Their words guide me as I learn to walk with Jesus every day.
Help me be a Barnabas. I want to encourage people in my life.
In the wonderful name of Jesus, I pray. Amen.

12

The Holy Spirit Gives Gifts

Memory Verse: There are different kinds of gifts,
but the same Spirit distributes them.
There are different kinds of service, but the same Lord.

1 CORINTHIANS 12:4–5 (NIV)

RAFTING DOWN THE RIVER

Have you ever ridden on a raft down a flowing river? That's an exciting adventure for vacationers in Colorado. With paddle in hand, you help move down the river, avoiding rocks and rapids. The river is running full, yet along the way small streams flow into it. The river also sends water into other small creeks. Ever receiving, ever passing on!

This is the way the Holy Spirit works in a believer's life. A *spiritual gift* is a God-given ability granted to individual believers by the Holy Spirit. This kind of gift allows believers to help others in their Christian walk.

WHAT ARE SOME SPIRITUAL GIFTS?

Romans 12:4–8* and 1 Peter 4:7–11# list some of these gifts. Find them by using the synonyms in the boxes. (Hint: Match the symbol after the Scripture passage in these directions to the symbol before the verse to find the answer.)

Preaching *Verse 6

P __ __ __ __ __ __ __ __ __ __

Educating *Verse 7

T __ __ __ __ __ __ __

Lifting Up *Verse 8

E __ __ __ __ __ __ __ __

Forgive *Verse 8

S __ __ __ M __ __ __ __

Entertain #Verse 9

H __ __ __ __ __ __ __ __ __ __

Talks #Verse 11

S __ __ __ __ __

Doing *Verse 7

S __ __ __ __ __ __

Offering *Verse 8

G __ __ __ __ __

Direct *Verse 8

L __ __ __

About spiritual gifts, the Bible says, *"All these are the work of one and the same Spirit, and he distributes them to each one, just as he determines."* 1 Corinthians 12:11 (NIV)

(Bonus: Paul lists more spiritual gifts for mature church leaders in 1 Corinthians 12:7–10.)

The First Gifts Were Given by Jesus Christ

Jesus gifted His followers with the special abilities each one would need to help build up the Church. These gifts equipped the believers to share the gospel, learn and grow in the faith, and become more like Jesus.

Read the Bible verse. Then fill in the blanks.

Ephesians 4:11–12 (NIV). *"So Christ himself gave the ________________, the ________________, the ____________________, the ____________ and ________________, to equip his people for works of service, so that the body of Christ may be built up."*

Answers on page 122

Spiritual Gifts vs. Natural Talents

Spiritual gifts are given by the Holy Spirit to believers. The purpose of these gifts is to get Christians ready to serve others. (See 1 Peter 4:10.)

Natural talent is the ability to do something well. Everyone everywhere is born with a talent or an interest in a special activity. Your talent might be sports, music, or drama. Maybe you are good at painting, cooking, or gardening. You may have received these talents from your parents or grandparents. Maybe you discovered an interest when trying different skills at school or clubs.

Study the chart below to learn about talents and possible gifts.

Biblical People, Their Talents, and Spiritual Gifts

Person	Natural Talent	Spiritual Gifts
David	*Sling-shot shooter, warrior, king*	*Writer of praise psalms*
Matthew	*Tax Collector*	*Teacher, author of Book of Matthew*
Peter	*Fisherman*	*Preacher, great church leader*
John	*Fisherman*	*Prophet, seeing visions, and writing Book of Revelation*
Dorcas	*Seamstress*	*Serving others, sharing*
Paul	*Tentmaker*	*Preacher, teacher, missionary*
Luke	*Physician*	*Missionary, historian, author*
Pricilla & Aquila	*Tentmakers*	*Co-workers with Paul, hospitality*
Jesus	*Carpenter*	*Teacher, Miracle-worker, Savior*

Are You Too Young to Receive a Spiritual Gift?

While many of these gifts have been given to mature Christians, many young people have received spiritual gifts.

1. Charles Spurgeon became a Christian as a teenager. He preached his first sermon at the age of 16. It soon became evident that God had given him the gift of preaching. He became famous, and many people throughout England became believers because of his ministry.

2. Franny Crosby wrote her first poem when she was eight years old. Despite being blind, she became a famous poet, song writer, and composer. She wrote more than 8,000 hymns. She dedicated her life to using the great gift the Holy Spirit had given her.
3. At 16 years of age, Billy Graham became a Christian at a revival in North Carolina. As a young man attending college in Florida, he felt called to preach. Sometimes Billy paddled a canoe to a small island in a nearby river. In the quietness of God's creation, he often practiced preaching to the birds, alligators, and stumps of Cypress trees. The Holy Spirit used Billy in a mighty way. From the time his adult ministry began in 1947, Graham conducted more than 400 crusades in 185 countries and territories on six continents.

Who Receives a Spiritual Gift?

As a young person, do you have a gift? When you were saved by Jesus Christ, the Holy Spirit came into your life. A gift was given to you at that time. The following verses are for all believers:

> *"Now to each one the manifestation of the Spirit is given for the common good."*
> 1 Corinthians 12:7 (NIV)

> *"We have different gifts, according to the grace given to each of us."*
> Romans 12:6 (NIV)

DISCUSSION

1. Have you ever tossed a pebble out onto a lake and watched how it sent wide circles or ripples far out, often reaching distant shores?
   How can this be like your influence when you use your spiritual gift?

2. If you don't already know, how can you discover what gift you have been given?
   a. Pray that God will guide you as you search for your gift.
   b. Be patient. God has a plan for your life. He will reveal it to you.
   c. Listen to your heart. What brings you joy when helping others?

APPLICATION

1. Complete the Chart:

Recognizing Talents vs. Gifts for Your Family

Start with your name. Fill in your talents. Wait to learn possible gifts. See if you can fill in the boxes for each member of your family.

Name	Talents	Possible Gifts
1.		
2.		
3.		
4.		
5.		

2. A Verse to Memorize. Copy the verse below on an index card. Underline or print important words (shown in bold print) in color to help you remember the verse. You may want to color-code this verse in your Bible as well.

Be ***strong*** *and* ***courageous****.*
Do not be ***afraid****;*
do not be ***discouraged****,*
for the LORD *your* ***God***
will be ***with*** *you* ***wherever*** *you go.*

Joshua 1:9 (NIV), emphasis added

PRAYER

Heavenly Father,
You are our Sovereign God
in charge of everything, including me.
I'm glad to know You have a plan for my life
and that You have a gift I can use to help other people.
Please show me what it is and how I can use it
to help other people and bring glory to Your name.
Thank You for (name recent blessings).
I'm so glad I belong to Your family.
In the name of Your Son, Jesus, amen.

13

The Holy Spirit Gives Hospitality

Memory Verse: Do not forget to show hospitality to strangers, for by so doing some people have shown hospitality to angels without knowing it.

HEBREWS 13:2 (NIV)

When you see a new person at church, what do you do?

A. Say hello and introduce yourself.

B. Offer to sit with him or her.

C. Help the new person find a classroom.

D. All of the above.

If you chose D, you showed someone hospitality!

WHAT IS HOSPITALITY?

One common definition of *hospitality* is giving a friendly, warm welcome to visitors or strangers.

Isaiah 58:7 (NIV) gives us a more detailed definition:

"Is it not to share your food with the hungry
and to provide the poor wanderer with shelter—
when you see the naked, to clothe them,
and not to turn away from your own flesh and blood?"

WHERE IT ALL BEGAN

Hospitality became a highly valued trait of the Jews early in their history. Many welcomed weary travelers or fed strangers. Out of these activities, the roots of the hospitality we offer to others today developed.

Hospitality: Given and Received

Read the Scriptures. Copy the correct animal into Columns 2 and 3.
Then color the animals.

Scripture	Who Offered It?	Who Received It?
Genesis 18:1–5 	*Martha*	*Elisha*
Genesis 24:26–34 	*King David*	*Jesus*
Exodus 2:15–22 	*Shunamite Woman*	*Lame Mephibosheth*
2 Samuel 9:1–10 	*Zacchaeus*	*Abraham's servant*
2 Kings 4:8–10 	*Abraham*	*Jesus and His disciples*
Luke 10:38–42 	*Reuel*	*3 Men at Mamre*
Luke 19:1–10 	*Laban*	*Moses*

Answers on page 123

READ A STORY

In the Book of Acts in the New Testament, we read about a wonderful couple who believed in Jesus and offered hospitality to those in need. Paul mentions them in his letters to the churches as well. Through their kindness and Christian witness, this faithful couple helped to spread the gospel and strengthen the foundation of the Church.

Aquila and Priscilla: A Caring Team

In about 50 AD the emperor issued a decree that forced all Jews to leave Rome. Aquila was a Jew who lived in Italy. He and his wife, Priscilla, boarded a ship for Corinth in Greece. (See Acts 18:1–2.)

When they arrived, Aquila and Priscilla searched for a small shop. They worked in their leather business together. They planned to set up their tentmaking shop on the street level. Then they would live upstairs.

One day another Jewish tentmaker arrived in town. Apostle Paul walked through the marketplace. He often looked for the chance to talk about Jesus. He met Aquila and Priscilla and visited with them in their shop. A deep friendship soon formed. The couple invited Paul to live with them and work in their shop. (See Acts 18:2–3.)

After a year and a half, Paul left for Ephesus. He took Priscilla and Aquila with him. (See Acts 18:18.) In Ephesus the couple opened their hearts to the young Christians living there. They started a church in their home. (See 1 Corinthians 16:19.)

One Sabbath in the synagogue, Priscilla and Aquila heard a great preacher. Apollos was an intelligent man with a deep knowledge of the old Scriptures. He knew about the baptism by John for the forgiveness of sins. However, his understanding was limited about the death of Jesus and the indwelling of the Holy Spirit. Priscilla and Aquila invited him into their home. They passed on what they had learned from Paul and helped build up Apollos in the faith. (See Acts 18:24–26.)

Later in Paul's travels, he wrote back to the church: *"Give my greetings to Priscilla and Aquila, my co-workers in the ministry of Christ Jesus."* (Romans 16:3 NLT)

To Do

Highlight or underline words or phrases in the story that you think show acts of hospitality.

CHALLENGE

A Linking Word Puzzle

Two words—HOSPITALITY and FOOD—are the only clues to help you solve this special puzzle. The rest of the words are found in Matthew 25:35–40 (NIV). Follow these suggestions.

1. Read the Scripture passage. If you are working with a group, others can follow along in their Bibles.
2. Someone announces what kind of word is needed.
   (For example: Find a 5-letter word that begins with "P.")
3. Look for that word. The first one who finds it says the word aloud and spells it, if necessary. Write the word in the puzzle where it belongs.
4. There are four more words that are linked to "Hospitality."
   Find those next. One word ends with a "Y." It has 6 letters.
5. Now continue with the challenge to complete the puzzle.

"If anyone ___________ even a _______ of cold _____________ to one of these ____________ ones who is my ________________, truly I tell you, that _______________ will ________________ not ________ their ______________." Matthew 10:42 (NIV)

Answers on page 123

DISCUSSION

How would you explain these statements about hospitality?

1. Hospitality is when someone feels at home in your presence.
2. People will forget what you said or what you did, but they will never forget how you made them feel.
3. Hospitality is simply an opportunity to show love and care.
4. "Offer hospitality to one another without grumbling." 1 Peter 4:9 (NIV)

APPLICATION

1. Everyone can practice hospitality even if you do not have that spiritual gift. Review your normal daily schedule. When and to whom could you offer extra kindness, love, friendship, or care? Make a list of possibilities. Then choose your first one to practice.
2. A Verse to Memorize. Copy the verse below on an index card. Underline or print important words (shown in bold print) in color to help you remember the verse. You may want to color-code this verse in your Bible as well.

*Do not **forget** to do **good***
*and to **share** with **others**,*
*for with such **sacrifices God** is **pleased**.*

Hebrews 13:16 (NIV)

PRAYER

Dear Heavenly Father,
You are a God of love, kindness, and caring.
I want to be more like You and practice hospitality.
Open my eyes so I can see possibilities
and offer hospitality without grumbling.
You have blessed me greatly, and I want to share with others.
I'm grateful for this lesson about helping others.
Help me live the way that pleases You.
In Jesus' wonderful name, amen.

14

The Holy Spirit Is the Spirit of Truth

Memory Verse: When he, the Spirit of truth, comes, he will guide you into all the truth. He will not speak on his own; he will speak only what he hears, and he will tell you what is yet to come.

JOHN 16:13 (NIV)

HOW IMPORTANT IS THE TRUTH?

Have you ever watched a TV court show? Each witness must repeat these words: "I swear to tell the truth, the whole truth, and nothing but the truth, so help me God."

The earthly value of telling the truth in court is so that you will not commit perjury (knowingly telling a lie) and be punished. The value of telling the truth in your school or in your home is that you won't have to remember what you already said to try and avoid punishment if you lie. The spiritual value of telling the truth is that you meet a requirement to get into heaven.

WHERE DOES THE SPIRIT OF TRUTH COME FROM?

Read the verse in your Bible. Then fill in the blanks.

John 14:16–17 (NIV). Jesus said: *"I will ________ the ________________, and he will ________ you another ______________ to help you and be with you ____________— the ____________ _____ ____________."*

Now we know that both the Father and the Son want to help us live by Jesus' teachings. They have sent the Holy Spirit. When we asked Jesus into our heart, the Holy Spirit entered and lives in us forever. He will be our teacher and guide as the following verses will show us.

Chief Functions of the Spirit of Truth

Read the following Scriptures. Look for verbs (action words) that begin each phrase that describes the Holy Spirit's important duties. Copy that phrase.

1. John 14:26a ______________________________
2. John 14:26b ______________________________

____

3. John 15:26 ______________________________
4. John 16:13a ______________________________
5. John 16:13b ______________________________
6. John 16:13c ______________________________
7. John 16:14 ______________________________
8. John 16:15b ______________________________
9. Ephesians 1:13b ______________________________

____

10. Ephesians 1:14 ______________________________

Summary

The ministry of the Holy Spirit is marked by love and action. He shares completely about the Son of God. He clarifies the teachings of Jesus. He honors and praises Jesus. He builds up the church body. He performs daily in the lives of individual believers.

That's His Job. What's Yours?

1. Read the Word.

Every teacher has a textbook. Every student needs to read and study the textbook. In this case the textbook is the Holy Bible. As you read the Bible daily, the Spirit can explain the verses and teach you truths that may be hidden below the surface. As you live each day and face difficult challenges, the Spirit can remind you of the lessons Jesus taught. He can bring to your mind the very verses that can get you through any rough spot.

2. Memorize the Word.

Your job is to hide God's Word in your heart. When we memorize Bible verses, we will always have them with us everywhere we go. Even if we don't have our Bible with us, we can remember what it says and share God's Word with others.

"Blessed is the one…whose ______________ is in the ________ of the LORD, and who ________________ on his law ___________ and ______________." Psalm 1:1–2 (NIV)

Answers on page 123

3. Listen and Obey the Spirit.

The Holy Spirit can speak to us through God's Word. As we read, certain verses may stand out to us. Suddenly, we understand something that God wants us to do. Other times, we realize we have been doing something that God does not want us to do. The Holy Spirit uses the truth of the Bible to help us follow Jesus, make wise choices, and stay on the right path.

CHALLENGE

Truth and **Falsehood** will be captains of two teams. Circle the words below in the puzzle. Then list them under the correct captain in the table on the next page. You may draw pictures of the captains.

Cheat	**Fake**	**Imitation**	**Pure**	**Sinful**
Crooked	**Genuine**	**Innocent**	**Real**	**Tricky**
Dependable	**Guilty**	**Lie**	**Right**	**Trustworthy**
Fact	**Honest**	**Pretend**	**Sincere**	**Two-faced**
Fair				**Wrong**

L A I N N O C E N T I G P V Y F K H H S B U N L S
S N X N I J O H N M O C K Z L M A W V E G G M I C
C I S V T Y D E J B W L N Z Y V N I W V R N N P F
M Z N G L S V O U R E K O K S Z T M R K I F O J G
Q L X C L F A E Z F P D F E U Y R G W V U K R R T
U T I Z E R S R D E P E N D A B L E I L Z E R D W
A C F E N R Z Z T O U T B P B E F M V M D G V K G
T A P E S L E W V W E W F F E O I G C P M L Q E X
R F N Y F U Z R B K O E Z M S T C X R T Q R N N T
Q M T C Y D I U A V P F A Y A V V I F S E U C T D
I F R R U H X F G R O Z A T P Z W E W A I E R U P
T Z G O K G T U I U S X I C M B X E L N Y S P T G
L D M O W A W R Q S D O V H E S D X E Q K I O A U
I N S K J E Y S O F N P C K D D M A V M Q H S L T
C I M E T W T D Q W W B D Y K N T J Z Y K C I R T
G H D D B R K R U F T T K H M S E M C K T J T T U
C U E W Z H G Q S B H S C Q E K M T U S U L C T G
U Z G A A I L G O G C S U N T V G Q E T E T I Y W
Z L K B T Q S F I G N E O R P M X M B R L V N U J
E Q T Q E Z V R F U A H L W T D A U U D P A U L G

Answers on page 123

TRUTH TEAM		FALSEHOOD TEAM	

DISCUSSION

1. In the middle of the day, has a Bible verse suddenly popped into your head? Perhaps, *"Love your neighbor as yourself"* (Matthew 22:39 NIV), or *"Do to others as you would have them do to you"* (Luke 6:31 NIV). This is the Spirit reminding you of Jesus' teachings. Share this experience with others in your family or group.
2. Jesus taught us how to worship God. Share your thoughts about this verse.

"God is spirit, and his worshipers must worship
in the Spirit and in truth." John 4:24 (NIV)

APPLICATION

1. How can you help the Holy Spirit "glorify Jesus" or "testify about Jesus?" Make a list of ideas—whatever comes into your mind.
2. A Verse to Memorize. Copy the verse below on an index card. Underline or print important words (shown in bold print) in color to help you remember the verse. You may want to color-code this verse in your Bible as well.

*I have **hidden** your **word** in my **heart***
*that I might not **sin** against you.*
***Praise** be to you, LORD.*

Psalm 119:11–12 (NIV), emphasis added

Answers on page 123

PRAYER

O Lord my God,
How great You are!
You are the source of all my joy,
and I will praise You every day.
Thank You for sending the Spirit of Truth
to be my teacher and guide.
I'm so glad He will help me recognize falsehood
if I see it in my school and community.
Show me how I can glorify Jesus, my Savior and Friend.
In the name of Jesus, the One who died for me, amen.

15

The Holy Spirit Can Be Grieved

Memory Verse: Do not grieve the Holy Spirit of God, with whom you were sealed for the day of redemption.

EPHESIANS 4:30 (NIV)

UNDERSTANDING WORDS

What does it mean to grieve the Holy Spirit?

- To "grieve" the Holy Spirit means to cause Him great distress, to sadden His Person, to wound His Spirit.
- To "quench" the Holy Spirit (see 1 Thessalonians 5:19) means to put out His fire, to suppress or stifle His Spirit.

READ A STORY

What happened in Bible times when someone grieved the Holy Spirit? Let's read one example based on Acts 4:34–35 and 5:1–10. If you are learning with your family or small group, you can assign readers to share this story aloud.

A Double Lie

Reader 1: From time to time, people who owned land or houses sold them. They brought the money from the sales and put it at the apostles' feet. It was distributed to anyone who had need.

Reader 2: A man named Ananias and his wife, Sapphira, had sold a piece of land. They agreed to keep back part of the price for themselves.

Reader 3: Ananias stood before Peter. He laid the rest of the money at the apostles' feet.

Reader 1: Peter said, "Ananias, why have you allowed Satan to fill your heart with evil? You lied to the Holy Spirit. You have kept some of the money for yourself."

Reader 2: Peter continued, "Didn't the land belong to you before it was sold? And after it was sold, wasn't the money all yours to decide what you would do with it?"

Reader 3: Ananias nodded his head in agreement.

Reader 1: "What made you think of keeping some for yourself?" Peter asked. "You not only lied to humans, but you lied to God."

Reader 3: When Ananias heard this, he fell down dead.

Reader 2: People were afraid when they heard what had happened.

Reader 1: Young men wrapped up his body. They carried him out and buried him.

Reader 3: About three hours later, Sapphira came in. She did not know what had happened.

Reader 1: Peter asked her a question, naming the price her husband quoted, "Is this the amount you and Ananias got when you sold your land?"

Reader 2: She answered, "Yes, that was the price."

Reader 3: Peter said, "Why did the two of you plot to test the Spirit of the Lord?"

Reader 1: "Listen!" Peter said. "Do you hear those footsteps? Those are the feet of the young men who just buried your husband for lying to the Holy Spirit. They will carry you out next."

Reader 2: She immediately fell dead at Peter's feet. The men carried her out and buried her next to her husband.

Reader 3: The whole church and all who heard the news were terrified about these events.

—The End—

Grieving is how the Spirit *feels and responds* to our actions, attitudes, and words that are opposite of what Jesus teaches and God desires.

Quenching the Spirit is *what we do* when we commit a wrongful act, harbor a hateful attitude, or speak harmful, evil words.

Remember, a definition for *quench* is "to put out," like you do to a campfire. You pour water on the fire to extinguish it so that it will not spread. The Holy Spirit is like a fire whose flame we **do not** want to put out.

Punishment for quenching the Holy Spirit does not usually result in instant death, like it did for Ananias and Sapphira. But we do need to repent if we have sinned like they did by disobeying or lying to God.

WHAT MAKES THE HOLY SPIRIT SAD?

Imagine what it would be like to be a parent. You love your kids so much! You do everything you can to keep them happy and healthy. You teach them important skills and try to protect them from harm. But even though you do your best to be a good parent, sometimes your kids don't listen. They make some serious mistakes and sinful choices. When you see them hurting and in trouble because of their disobedience, you are sad.

Like a parent loves a child, the Holy Spirit wants what is best for us. When we disobey God, the Holy Spirit grieves over us.

Actions That Cause the Holy Spirit to Grieve

Read the following verses and match them to the sins against the Holy Spirit. Some verses will be used more than once. Write the alphabet letter of the verse in the first column. Some are challenging.

A. Ephesians 4:25
B. Ephesians 4:28
C. Ephesians 4:29
D. Ephesians 4:31
E. Ephesians 5:3
F. Ephesians 5:4
G. Hebrews 13:16

Letter	Actions That Cause the Holy Spirit to Grieve
	Anger
	Rage
	Lying, telling falsehoods
	Stealing
	Telling dirty or coarse jokes
	Greed
	Selfishness
	Bitterness
	Unwholesome talk (verbally tearing one another down)
	Brawling, fighting
	Sexual misconduct
	Obscenity (bad language)

Answers on page 123

CHALLENGE

Join the Bee Club

Think about how to please the Holy Spirit with the positive actions you could do and the kind words you could speak.

Then see how many things you can write on the alphabet list below. Begin each with "Be...." You can write more than one word or phrase per letter. Perhaps you can have a contest with other family members or friends.

A. Be Amiable

B. ____________________

C. ____________________

D. ____________________

E. ____________________

F. ____________________

G. ____________________

H. ____________________

I. ____________________

J. ____________________

K. ____________________

L. ____________________

M. ____________________

N. ____________________

O. ____________________

P. ____________________

Q. ____________________

R. ____________________

S. ____________________

T. ____________________

U. ____________________

V. ____________________

W. ____________________

X. ____________________

Y. ____________________

Z. ____________________

When you have finished your list, highlight qualities you believe you have. Underline traits you would like to work on.

Answers on page 123

DISCUSSION

1. The Bible says in 1 John 1:9 (NIV), *"If we confess our sins, he is faithful and just and will forgive us our sins and purify us from all unrighteousness."* This verse has been called the "Christians' Bar Soap." Apply as often as necessary.

2. This is a good time to confess anything you have done wrong. Pray for yourself and for one another.

APPLICATION

1. Make this chart for a wall in your room.

BEFORE YOU SPEAK, THINK!

T — Is it Truthful?
H — Is it Helpful?
I — Is it Inspiring?
N — Is it Necessary?
K — Is it Kind?

2. Verses to Memorize. Copy the verses below on an index card. Underline or print important words (shown in bold print) in color to help you remember the verse. You may want to color-code this verse in your Bible as well.

(Young children can choose a shorter part to memorize.)

Shout for joy to the ***LORD****, all the* ***earth****.*
Worship *the LORD with* ***gladness****;*
come *before him with joyful* ***songs****.*
Know *that the LORD is* ***God****.*
It is he who ***made*** *us, and we are his;*
we are his ***people****, the* ***sheep*** *of his* ***pasture****.*

Enter *his gates with* ***thanksgiving***
and his courts with ***praise****;*
give ***thanks*** *to him and praise his* ***name****.*

For the LORD is ***good*** *and his love endures* ***forever****;*
his ***faithfulness*** *continues through all* ***generations****.*

Psalm 100:1–5 (NIV), emphasis added

PRAYER (Use the words of a psalm.)

I praise You, Heavenly Father.
Yours is the greatness and the power
and the glory and the majesty and the splendor.
Everything in heaven and earth is Yours.
In Your hands is power to give strength
to those who call upon Your name.
You are a wonderful God, and I honor you.
Thank You for the way You have answered my prayers
and helped my family through tough spots. (Name some.)
I learned a lot about the Holy Spirit, who lives inside me.
Now I understand that He is a Person with feelings.
I will try to please Him with my actions and words.
In the name of Jesus, the precious Son of God, amen.

16

The Holy Spirit Gives Peace

Memory Verse: Peace I leave with you; my peace I give you.
I do not give to you as the world gives.
Do not let your hearts be troubled and do not be afraid.

JOHN 14:27 (NIV)

WHAT IS PEACE?

What do you think of when you hear the word *peace*? Maybe you think of a beautiful place you have seen: a mountain, forest, or ocean. Maybe you remember a sound you have heard like the chirp of crickets, the soft clank of a cowbell, or the rush of wind through the leaves. Maybe you are reminded of a fragrance like newly mown grass, a bouquet of flowers, or your mom's freshly baked chocolate chip cookies. All these things can be described as peaceful.

THE GIVER OF REAL PEACE

The peace the Holy Spirit gives is so much more than the things we have just mentioned. His peace isn't based on or affected by what we experience on the outside. The Holy Spirit living inside us is the source of real peace that nothing in the world can take away.

What did Paul write to the Thessalonian church about peace? Read the verse to fill in the blanks.

2 Thessalonians 3:16 (NIV) *"Now may the __________ of ____________ himself __________ you ____________at _________ ___________ and in _________________ __________. The __________ be ____________ all of you."*

READ A STORY

Our story today is about a fearless servant of God. As you read, look up the scriptures in your Bible. Then fill in the blanks.

Meet Stephen
(Based on Acts 6 and 7)

Stephen was a deacon. He and six other men were chosen to be in charge of the daily distribution of food to the poor.

Stephen was a man full of faith, wisdom, and the Holy Spirit. Stephen was also *"full of God's grace and* ______________." This allowed him to perform *"great* ______________ *and signs among the people."* (Acts 6:8 NIV)

Members of a unique synagogue, called the Freedmen, didn't like Stephen or his preaching. They tried to argue with him about his teachings. However, they could not compete with the wisdom that the Holy Spirit gave Stephen. (Acts 6:10)

The Freedmen's hate for Stephen was so strong that they persuaded some men to testify against him. These men said, *"We have heard Stephen speak blasphemous words against* ______________ *and against* _________." (Acts 6:11 NIV)

Hatred spread. Elders and teachers of the law joined in. They seized Stephen and took him before the Sanhedrin. They also produced false witnesses who said Stephen spoke against Jewish law and said that the teachings of Jesus would destroy the temple and teachings of Moses.

Everyone in the Sanhedrin looked intently at Stephen. What they saw was a very peaceful man. They saw that his face "________ ________ ________ ___________ _____ _____ ______________." (Acts 6:15 NIV)

The high priest asked Stephen, *"Are these charges true?"* (Acts 7:1)

Stephen did not defend himself. Instead, he began giving a long summary about the Jewish history. He told how the Jews had rejected God's message and His messengers. (Acts 7:2–50).

Stephen's Testimony about Jewish History in the Old Testament

Read Acts chapter 7 to find the answers. At the end of each clue, the V followed by a number tells you which verse to read to find the answer.

Across

4. The father of the 12 Patriarchs. (V. 8)
6. Who refused to obey Moses and yearned to go back to Egypt? (V. 39)
8. Son of Abraham. (V. 8)
11. He led the people with the Tabernacle into land God directed. (V. 44–45)
12. He was reared by Pharaoh's daughter and educated in the palace. (V. 21–22)
13. Moses lived here for 40 years. (V. 29)
14. God promised that this man and his descendants would possess the land. (V. 5)

Down

1. He made a golden idol in the form of a calf for the people to worship. (V. 40–41)
2. What men were jealous of Joseph and sold him into slavery? (V. 9)
3. Where did God first appear to Abraham? (V. 2)
5. Who appeared in a burning bush to Moses? (V. 30)
7. God sent Moses back to this country to free the Israelites. (V. 34)
9. God gave him wisdom and ability to gain the good will of Pharaoh. (V. 10)
10. He enjoyed God's favor. (V. 45–46)

Answers on page 124

Stephen Condemned the Present Jews

(Based on Acts 7:51–60)

Stephen said, "You stubborn people! You are physically Jews, that's true. But your hearts and minds are no different than the Gentiles. You are just like your ancestors—you constantly fight against the Holy Spirit! Can you name a prophet your ancestors did not torture? They even killed the prophets who foretold the coming of the Messiah. And you have betrayed and murdered Jesus Christ."

Find and read the verses in Acts 7 to fill in the blanks.

Verse 54. How did the Jews respond when they heard this? ____________________

____

Verse 55. *"But Stephen, full of the Holy Spirit,* ____________________

____

____

Verse 56. What did Stephen say? " ____________________

____."

Verses 57–58. What five things did the Jews do next?

1. ____________________
2. ____________________
3. ____________________
4. ____________________
5. ____________________

Verse 59. While they were stoning him, Stephen prayed, " ____________________

____."

Verse 60. Then he fell on his knees and cried out, " ____________________

____."

Verse 60. Then he fell asleep.

CHALLENGE

Read the definitions of peace. Next to the scriptures you wrote out in the story above, write the letters in the margin that describe the type of peace Stephen was experiencing.

Definitions of Peace: **a.** freedom from disturbance; **b.** calmness; **c.** heart at rest; **d.** wholeness of mind and spirit; **e.** tranquility

Evidence of the Holy Spirit at Work

Draw the correct symbol in the box that matches the Verse and the Holy Spirit's Action.

Reference	Verse	Holy Spirit's Action
Acts 6:5 	*Then he fell on his knees and cried out, "Lord, do not hold this sin against them."*	Comforter—(glorifies Jesus)
Acts 6:10 	*When he had said this, he fell asleep.*	Can be grieved
Acts 6:15 	*Stephen, full of the Holy Spirit, looked up to heaven and saw the glory of God, and Jesus standing at the right hand of God.*	Gives peace
Acts 7:51 	*"Look," he said, "I see heaven open and the Son of Man standing at the right hand of God."*	Leads (guides)
Acts 7:55 	*All who were sitting in the Sanhedrin looked intently at Stephen, and they saw that his face was like the face of an angel.*	Empowers to witness
Acts 7:56 	*They could not stand up against the wisdom the Spirit gave him as he spoke.*	Helps us forgive others
Acts 7:60 	*They chose Stephen, a man full of faith and of the Holy Spirit.*	Gives peace
Acts 7:60 	*You are just like your ancestors: You always resist the Holy Spirit!*	Gives wisdom

Answers on page 124

DISCUSSION

Think or talk about when and where you may have experienced any of these definitions of peace or when you wish you could have:

calmness, silence, tranquility, restfulness, quietness, silence, stillness, seclusion, freedom from disturbance, freedom from interference, privacy, noiselessness

APPLICATION

1. Choose a quiet, secluded place where you can read your Bible and talk to God.
2. A Verse to Memorize. Copy the verse below on an index card. Underline or print important words (shown in bold print) in color to help you remember the verse. You may want to color-code this verse in your Bible as well.

How to Maintain Peace

Bear *with each other*
and ***forgive*** *one* ***another***
if any of you has a ***grievance*** *against* ***someone****.*
Forgive *as the* ***Lord*** *forgave* ***you****.*

Colossians 3:13 (NIV), emphasis added

PRAYER

Dear Heavenly Father,
I praise You for Your many qualities, O God.
You are present everywhere,
always listening to my prayers,
and always watching over me.
Thank You for Your perfect plan of salvation
and for sending Your Son Jesus to forgive me of my sins.
Thank You for sending the Holy Spirit to live within me.
I'm grateful that He shows me Your will
and reminds me of the teachings of Jesus.
One of His greatest gifts is peace.
I've learned much about the peace He gives.
I ask You to bless my family tonight.
In the name of Jesus, Your Beloved Son, I pray. Amen.

17

The Holy Spirit Strengthens

Memory Verse: May our Lord Jesus Christ himself and God our Father...encourage your hearts and strengthen you in every good deed and word.

2 THESSALONIANS 2:16–17 (NIV)

When you want strong muscles, what do you do? You go to the gym, you exercise your muscles, and you grow stronger. Sometimes those muscles may hurt a little, but you keep trying because the result will be worth it. The same is true when we persevere to grow spiritually. We need the Holy Spirit's help to make our faith strong.

JOB, A MAN OF GOD

The Book of Job in the Old Testament tells the story of a wealthy and upright man who suffered terrible persecution. Despite shocking losses, Job remained steadfast. He persevered through many trials and the criticism of his wife and friends.

Find the Book of Job in your Bible. Then read chapter 1:1–3 (NIV) and fill in the blanks.

In the land of _______, there lived a man whose name was ________.

He was ___________________ and ___________________;

he ______________ God and ___________________ evil.

He had ___________ sons and __________ daughters.

He owned _____________ sheep, _______________ camels, _____________ yoke of

_________ and 500 ________________, and had many servants.

He was the __________________ man among all the people of the ____________.

READ A PLAY

This play summarizes the story of Job's life. Even when he didn't understand why so many bad things were happening to him, Job kept his strong faith in God. He never gave up. What happened to Job in the end?

As you read this play, look for sentences that describe Job's faith. If you are reading this play with your family or group, you can choose a different reader for each part. If not, you can read all the parts yourself.

A Conversation Between Satan and God

CAST:

Narrator—storyteller who describes the actions and settings

God—the Almighty Creator of everything

Satan—an angel who rebelled against God

Job—a wealthy man who loves and serves God

Wife—married to Job

Scene—A meeting in heaven and corresponding events on earth in the land of Uz

Narrator: The angels had come for a meeting with God. Satan came along with them.

God: Where have you come from, Satan?

Satan: I've been roaming around the earth, looking at Your people.

God: Have you noticed my servant Job? There is no one on earth like him. He is faultless and honorable. He worships Me and avoids evil in all his daily activities.

Satan: No wonder. You put a hedge of protection around him, his family, and his flocks. You have blessed all he does. But stretch out Your hand and strike everything he has. I'm sure he will curse You to Your face.

God: Very well. I will put everything he has in your hands. But you must not lay a finger on Job himself.

Narrator: One day, several messengers reported to Job that all his cattle were stolen, and some were burned alive. All his servants were killed.

Narrator: Then another messenger came and said, "Your sons and daughters were feasting at the oldest brother's house when a mighty wind swept in from the desert. It struck the four corners of the house. The house collapsed, and all your children are dead."

Job stood, tore his robe, and shaved his head. He fell to the ground in worship and said —

Job: "*Naked I came from my mother's womb, and naked I will depart. The LORD gave and the LORD has taken away; may the name of the LORD be praised.*" (Job 1:21 NIV)

Narrator: On another day, the angels were presenting themselves to God again. Satan appeared too.

God: Where have you come from, Satan?

Satan: From roaming through the earth, looking around at Your creation.

God: Certainly, you have watched my servant Job. He is an honorable man. Though you provoked Me against him to ruin him for no reason, he still behaves in an honorable way.

Satan: Skin for skin! A man will give all he has for his own life. I dare You to stretch out Your hand and strike his flesh and bones. He will surely curse You to Your face.

God: Very well! He is in your hands, but you must spare his life.

Narrator: So, Satan left with a wicked plan. He covered Job with painful sores from the top of his head to the bottom of his feet.

Wife: Just look at you, Job! Sitting among the ashes and scraping your sores with a piece of broken pottery. Are you still trying to live a good and honest life? Curse God and die!

Job: You are talking like a foolish woman. Shall we accept good from God, and not trouble?

Narrator: In all his trouble, Job did not sin in what he said or did.

Later, three of Job's friends came to comfort him, but after many days they began preaching to him. They said, "You are suffering because you have sinned. You must confess your sins to God and then He will heal you."

Job: I will not deny my trust in God. *"To God belong wisdom and power; counsel and understanding are his."* (Job 12:13 NIV)

Strength and victory come from God. *"Though he slay me, yet will I hope in him."* (Job 13:15 NIV)

Narrator:	For many days (*and for 42 chapters!*), the debate continued. Job persevered and kept his faith. Finally, God spoke to Job. Then He spoke to Job's friends.
God:	I am angry with you men because you have not spoken of Me correctly. Job has remained faithful in spite of his suffering. Go offer a burnt sacrifice for yourselves. Then Job will pray for you, and I will accept his prayer and not deal with you according to your foolishness. (Job 42:7–9)
Narrator:	After Job prayed for his friends, God made him wealthy again. God gave Job twice as much as he had before. And God gave him seven new sons and three daughters, more beautiful than those before. God blessed him with a happy and long life. Job lived to see his grandchildren to the fourth generation.

—The End—

Complete the Bible verse to read what James in the New Testament said about Job.

"As you know, we count as ________________ those who have ____________________. You have heard of Job's ______________________ and have seen what the Lord finally brought about. The Lord is full of ________________________ and ______________." James 5:11 (NIV)

STRENGTH THROUGH PERSEVERANCE

Persevering through hard times is not easy, but that is how we become strong. The Bible has a lot to say about perseverance. This is what James said: *"Consider it pure joy, my brothers and sisters, whenever you face trials of many kinds, because you know that the testing of your faith produces perseverance."* (James 1:2–3 NIV)

Perseverance

Find and circle these synonyms of perseverance. Words may be hidden forwards, backwards, up, down, or diagonally.

Backbone	**Diligence**	**Guts**	**Pluck**
Bravery	**Endure**	**Nerve**	**Spunk**
Courage	**Firmness**	**Patience**	**Steadfastness**
Dedication	**Grit**	**Persistence**	**Strength**
Determined			**Toughness**

P G K Q A A M X M R Z H D U T R Y N H Y T L O K E
D Z D B T Y J Y Y W S P N F S J S O M E G Z Z N S
D E X W Q F E N N B F Z I L P T U A N Z X B D Y S
B V D O W T N D F J E S X W Y B R Y J F O U X C I
A P U I Z F E I D B L U A Y F J V E X A R J C J S
C N G F C V U Z W H Q W S G K W R C N E X U B Y S
K Q M M R A Z X B V R Q Y B U S D J V G B M X W E
B S L E Z J T I X H K H W S U T J R M N T F P M N
O U N O R D Z I C T A A O T F M S Y M Z N H G Y H
N E R Y B P E P O B J A L I S S E N M R I F Y G G
E H E A J M B T B N F Z W I E N S Z K C U L P O U
C Z C C V X G K E H X Z P V Q C O Z H I W Q T K O
N A J Q N U N R N R T N E L O G N D U M F H E W T
U X U D C E V A H M M O L C W X C E Y V F M W I C
A G Z T O P I Y G X V I N P N F E M T J H O X O C
P S I P Q U R T G A D A N C V E O C I S U P U P M
M Y D H K E U E A G N I E E E B G H N Z I R S T H
D K D N V V M A J P K I H B D L P I A T A S T Q T
Z I U A T Q X W M F V J U B I O Y C L G I Q R W L
Z P R O Q Y M L I C I O W F O L K Y E I M R K E H
S B M O J I W S T E A D F A S T N E S S D C G O P

Answers on page 124

Did the Son of God need to be strengthened?

Jesus lived on earth in human flesh. How did He receive strength to face His problems?

Read the Bible verses. Then fill in the blanks.

Luke 5:16 (NIV). *"Jesus often withdrew to lonely places and ________________."*

Jesus was in the wilderness, praying and fasting. He was weak from 40 days without food and from fighting three temptations by the devil. What happened next?

Matthew 4:11 (NIV). *"Then the devil left him, and ________________ came and attended him."*

Before Jesus faced trials, torture, and the crucifixion, He prayed in the Garden of Gethsemane.

Luke 22:42–43 (NIV). *"'Father, if you are willing, take this cup from me; yet not my will, but yours be done.' An ____________ from ________________ appeared to him and ________________________ him."*

Paul prayed for us to be strengthened.

Paul wrote to the church at Colossae: We pray for you *"so that you may live a life worthy of the Lord and please him in every way: ______________ fruit in every good work, ________________in the knowledge of God, being ______________________ with all _______________ according to his glorious might so that you may have great ____________________ and ________________."* Colossians 1:10–11 (NIV)

Prayer is our Power
and our Connection to God
to receive Strength so that
we can Endure all Trials and Temptations.

When trouble comes, some people turn away from God. They try to solve their problems on their own. Through our study of Job today, we see that God can bring good things out of our troubles when we persevere and hold on tightly to our faith. Being a Christian does not mean that life will always be easy or that things will always go our way. But we know we do not face trials on our own. As we pray and read the Bible, like Jesus and Paul did, the Holy Spirit gives us the strength and power we need.

CHALLENGE

Strengthened by the Holy Spirit

Use the code to read these encouraging Bible verses.

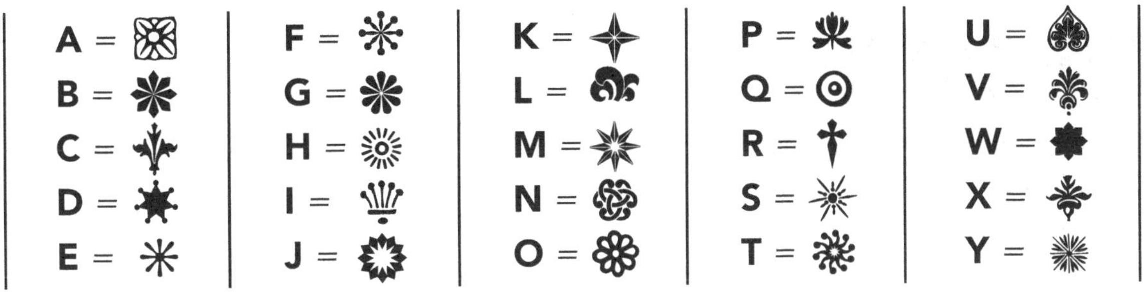

1. "I pray that out of his glorious riches he may strengthen you with ___ ___ ___ ___ ___

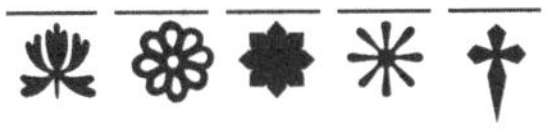

through his ___ ___ ___ ___ ___ ___ in your inner being."

2. "Consider it pure joy...whenever you face trials of many kinds, because you know that the testing of your faith

___ ___ ___ ___ ___ ___ ___ ___ ___ ___ ___ ___ ___ ___ ___ ___ ___ ___ ___ ___."

3. "I can do all this through him who

___ ___ ___ ___ ___ ___ ___ ___ ___ ___ ___ ___ ___ ___ ___."

4. "God is faithful.... When you are tempted, he will also provide a way out so that you

___ ___ ___ ___ ___ ___ ___ ___ ___ ___ ___."

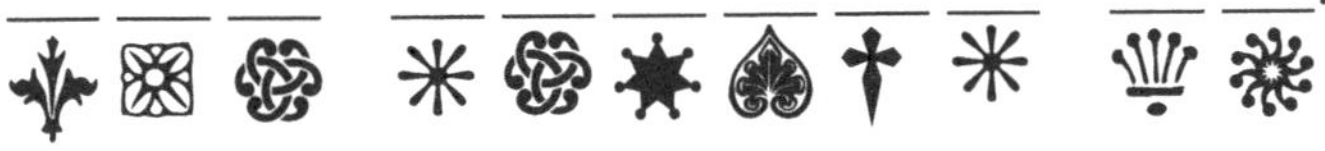

Scriptures for above puzzles:

1. Ephesians 3:16 (NIV)
2. James 1:2–3 (NIV)
3. Philippians 4:13 (NIV)
4. 1 Corinthians 10:13 (NIV)

Answers on page 124

DISCUSSION

1. How do you think Job was able to remain faithful to God in spite of his terrible losses and persecution from his friends and wife?
2. Have you been persecuted because of your Christian walk? How did you respond?

APPLICATION

1. Start a list of scriptures that the Holy Spirit can use to strengthen you in times of trouble.
2. A Verse to Memorize. Copy the verse below on an index card. Underline or print important words (shown in bold print) in color to help you remember the verse. You may want to color-code this verse in your Bible as well.

*The **eternal God** is your **refuge**,*
*and underneath are the **everlasting arms**.*

Deuteronomy 33:27 (NIV), emphasis added

PRAYER

Heavenly Father,
You are a loving and gracious God,
slow to get angry and abounding in patience.
Thank You, God, for the amazing deeds
You have done in the past and for Your blessings
that I see today. (Can you name one?)
I was glad to learn of Job's strength and faithfulness.
His life is a great example for me to follow.
I will trust in the Holy Spirit to strengthen me.
I want to be strong when friends try to get
me to do things I know will not please You.
I love and appreciate You, Lord.
I will honor and praise Your holy name.
In the name of Your Son who saves my soul, amen.

18

The Holy Spirit Intercedes

Memory Verse: The Spirit helps us in our weakness.
We do not know what we ought to pray for,
but the Spirit himself intercedes for us through wordless groans.

ROMANS 8:26 (NIV)

EVERYDAY INTERCESSORS

Sometimes people find themselves in difficult situations. The problem is too big or too confusing to solve alone. They need someone to help them, an intercessor, who will speak to the one in charge on their behalf.

Read these examples. Write the name on the line of someone you think would be the helper in each situation.

A) Daniel is being bullied at school. He told the bully to stop, and he tries to stay away from him. The bullying is still happening. Daniel is afraid to go to the principal by himself.

Who can help him? ______________________________

B) Emily got sick and is in the hospital. Her mom is right by her side, and she thinks Emily's fever is going up. Emily might need some medicine, but her doctor is off duty for the night.

Who can help Emily's mom reach the doctor? ______________________________

UNDERSTANDING WORDS

What does the word *intercede* mean?

Intercede means to beg or plead on behalf of someone else.
Intercede is a verb: *inter* means "between" and *cede* means "to go."

THE HOLY SPIRIT INTERCEDES FOR US

The Holy Spirit goes between the believer and God and makes our requests known to God.

In our helplessness, we often do not know the right words to say. The weight of our burden might be so heavy on our heart we can't even speak. That's when the Spirit comes to our rescue and prays for us. The Bible explains what the Holy Spirit does for us.

Read Romans 8:26–27 (NIV). Then fill in the blanks.

> *"The Spirit helps us in our ________________. We do not know what we ought to ____________ for, but the Spirit himself ________________________ for us through wordless _______________. And he who __________________ our _______________ knows the _______________ of the __________________, because the Spirit ___________________________ for God's ________________ in accordance with the _____________ of __________."*

PEOPLE CAN ALSO INTERCEDE FOR OTHERS

The Bible gives many examples of leaders who interceded with God on behalf of their people. Two men in the Old Testament who stood in the gap for others in an amazing way are Moses and Nehemiah.

Moses Intercedes for the Israelites

As you work this crossword puzzle, you will learn about a time when Moses interceded with God for his people. See if you can answer these questions:

1) What was the problem? **2)** What did Moses do? **3)** How did God respond?

Read Exodus 15:22–25 (NIV). Then complete the puzzle below.

Across

3. They traveled ___ days without water.

4. The water at Marah was ___.

7. The people ___ against Moses.

8. Moses led Israel from the __ Sea.

9. The LORD showed Moses a piece of __.

Down

1. They went into the Desert of ____.

2. Moses __ out to the LORD.

5. Moses __ it into the water.

6. The water became fit to __.

Answers on page 124

READ A STORY

Nehemiah, a Man of Prayer

(Based on Nehemiah 1—2)

As a Jewish servant, Nehemiah was the personal cupbearer to King Artaxerxes. His duty was to ensure the safety and quality of the king's food and drink.

Nehemiah loved his homeland. But because of the exile, he had lived his whole life in Babylon. Jerusalem was the Jew's holy city. He hoped to go there some day and worship in the temple.

One day Hanani and some other men from Judah came to visit Nehemiah. He questioned them about the Jewish people who were now living in Jerusalem.

Hanani answered, "Those who survived the exile are in great trouble and disgrace. The wall of Jerusalem is broken down. Its gates have been burned with fire."

Nehemiah sat down and wept. He mourned for many days, fasting and praying to God.

Nehemiah called out to God in three intercessory prayers.

Read the verses in the Bible. Then fill in the blanks.

1. Nehemiah 1:5–6 (NIV). *"LORD, the God of ____________, the great and ______________ God, who keeps his covenant of love with those who ___________ him and keep his commandments, let your ear be _________________ and your eyes __________ to hear the prayer your _________________ is praying before you day and night for your ________________, the people of ___________."*

2. Nehemiah 1:11 (NIV). *"Lord, let your _________ be attentive to the ______________ of this __________ __________________.... Give your servant _______________ today by _________________him ____________ in the _________________of this man* [the king]."

3. When Nehemiah took wine to the king, the king asked why he looked so sad. Nehemiah was very afraid, but he said to the king:

Nehemiah 2:3–5 (NIV). *"Why should my ____________not look sad when the city where my _________________are buried lies in ___________, and its gates have been destroyed by __________?"*

The king asked, *"What is it you __________?"*

Then Nehemiah prayed to God before answering the king. *"If it ______________ the king and if your ________________ has found _____________ in his sight, let him send me to the city in Judah...so that I can ______________ it."*

God answered Nehemiah's prayer. Nehemiah received permission from the king to go to Judah to restore the wall of Jerusalem.

—The End—

Some Special Instructions from Paul

We can read Paul's letter to Timothy in the New Testament. In it, Paul explains how important it is for Christians to intercede for others in our prayers. Our prayers can bring about peace as well as open doors for people around the world to hear and believe the truth of the gospel.

"I urge, then, first of all, that petitions,
prayers, intercession and thanksgiving
be made for all people—
for kings and all those in authority,
that we may live peaceful and
quiet lives in all godliness and holiness.
This is good, and pleases God our Savior,
who wants all people to be saved and
to come to a knowledge of the truth."

1 Timothy 2:1–4 (NIV)

Prayers of Jesus Christ

Jesus Christ is the greatest intercessor of them all. We have many examples of how Jesus prayed for people He knew on earth long ago and for Christians like us who are living now.

Unscramble the letters to read some of Jesus' intercessory prayers as well as a verse about what Jesus is able to do for us. Look up the verses in an NIV Bible to check your answers.

1. "I have ___ ___ ___ ___ ___ ___ for you, Simon, that ___ ___ ___ ___
   D R E A P Y — U R O Y

   ___ ___ ___ ___ ___ may not ___ ___ ___ ___." Luke 22:32 (NIV)
   H I T A F — A L I F

2. "I pray also for those who will ___ ___ ___ ___ ___ ___ ___ in ___ ___." John 17:20 (NIV)
   E V I E B E L — E M

3. "Father, ___ ___ ___ ___ ___ ___ ___ ___ ___ ___ ___, for they do not
   G R O V I F E — E H T M

   ___ ___ ___ ___ ___ ___ ___ ___ they are ___ ___ ___ ___ ___." Luke 23:34 (NIV)
   W N O K — T H A W — N I D O G.

4. Jesus "is able to ___ ___ ___ ___ completely those who come to ___ ___ ___ through
   V A S E — O D G

   him, because he always ___ ___ ___ ___ ___ to ___ ___ ___ ___ ___ ___ ___ ___ ___ for
   S L I E V — T E N E C R I E D

   ___ ___ ___ ___." Hebrews 7:25 (NIV)
   H E M T

DISCUSSION

1. Think or talk about Nehemiah's three prayers.
   What made them intercessory prayers?
2. When have you needed someone to intercede for you?
   How do you feel now that you know the Holy Spirit brings your needs before God?

Answers on page 124

APPLICATION

1. God needs prayer warriors today more than ever. Every believer can become active in this special kind of ministry. When you pray, remember to place the needs of others before your own needs. Who can you intercede for in your prayers? Make a list of people you can pray for.

2. A Verse to Memorize. Copy the verse below on an index card. Underline or print important words (shown in bold print) in color to help you remember the verse. You may want to color-code this verse in your Bible as well.

God's ***love*** *has been* ***poured*** *out*
into our ***hearts*** *through the Holy* ***Spirit****,*
who has been ***given*** *to us.*

Romans 5:5 (NIV), emphasis added

PRAYER

Dear Heavenly Father,
Holy is Your name.
You are powerful, patient, and perfect.
I honor Your name and worship You.
I am so glad the Holy Spirit prays for me
and tells You what I need.
I want to intercede for our president and leaders.
Please give them wisdom as they lead our country.
I ask that the Holy Spirit will teach me how to pray for others
like Your Son and Nehemiah did.
In the name of Jesus Christ, my Savior, amen.

19

The Holy Spirit Speaks to Us

Memory Verse: When he, the Spirit of truth, comes, he will guide you into all the truth. He will not speak on his own; he will speak only what he hears, and he will tell you what is yet to come.

JOHN 16:13 (NIV)

THE HOLY SPIRIT LIVES WITHIN EVERY BELIEVER

A very important function of the Holy Spirit is to communicate with us. He reveals the Heavenly Father's plan for our lives. And He can do this in many ways. In Bible times, He spoke to people through visions, dreams, and prophesies. Today, He speaks to us through different methods.

1. The Holy Bible

One of the most common methods the Holy Spirit uses to speak to us is through the Word of God—the Bible. That's why it is so important to read the Bible every day. First, the Holy Spirit helps us to understand what we read. Later, He will teach us truths by reminding us of the words of Jesus, the apostles, and Old Testament leaders.

Read 2 Timothy 3:16–17 (NIV). Then fill in the blanks.

"All ____________________ is __________-____________________ and is useful for ________________, rebuking, __________________ and ______________________ in righteousness, so that the __________________ of God may be thoroughly __________________ for every good ____________."

Something to Think About

Sometimes you are encouraged to read your Bible through in a year. However, speed is not always good if you want the Holy Spirit to reveal truths about the Scriptures. Take your time. Read a verse. Think about what it meant when it was first written.

The Holy Spirit guides us to understand what the author had in mind when he wrote each verse. Ask the Holy Spirit to reveal what the verses can mean to you. Meditate about a verse, a phrase, a word.

Give the Holy Spirit time to speak to you. Tell the Holy Spirit when you do not understand a verse. He may reveal its meaning to you now…or perhaps next month or next year.

2. Pastors, Evangelists, and Teachers

Another way the Holy Spirit speaks to us is through our church leaders. The pastor's Sunday sermons or the evangelist's special messages can give you new insights. The Sunday school teacher, who explains the Bible lessons every week, can make the Scriptures come alive to you.

Read Ephesians 4:11–12 (NIV). Then fill in the blanks.

> *"So Christ himself gave the ______________, the prophets, the ______________, the ______________ and teachers, to ____________ his people for works of service."*

How can you receive benefits from these speakers?

Lay aside any distraction like your iPhone with messages you may be reading or games you are playing. Be an attentive listener so the Holy Spirit can speak to you.

3. The Witness Within

When you first asked Jesus to come into your heart, the Holy Spirit came to live with you forever. You are a temple of the Holy Spirit. He actually dwells within you. He teaches you to know God and follow Him.

Read Romans 8:16 (NIV). Then fill in the blanks.

> *"The Spirit himself ______________ with our spirit that we are God's ______________."*

You will not hear an audible voice, but you will know without a doubt that the Holy Spirit is speaking to you. His Spirit bears witness with your spirit. When He speaks you will know what is true. Like seeing a bright light shining in the darkness, suddenly you will be able to understand the true meaning of the Scriptures.

Find John 15:26 (NIV) in your Bible and fill in the blanks.

> Jesus said, *"When the ________________ comes, whom I will send to you from the Father—the Spirit of truth who goes out from the Father—he will ________________ about me."*

4. Leadings

The Holy Spirit can give you direct messages. He can also show you what to do or not to do. A good example of this leading is found in Matthew 4:1 (NIV).

Read the verse and fill in the blanks.

> *"Then Jesus was __________ by the _______________ into the wilderness to be tempted by the devil."*

We can describe this leading with different terms. Some have called this leading a "feeling" or "impression." Some call it a "prompting." The Holy Spirit may speak to you with a gentle nudging or a strong pushing that you can't deny. These promptings can lead you forward, or they may stop your progress in a direction you should not be going.

God leads by putting His directions into our hearts.

One example of this is found in the story of Nehemiah.

> *"Now the city was large and spacious, but there were few people in it, and the houses had not yet been rebuilt. So my God put it into my heart to assemble the nobles...."* Nehemiah 7:4–5 (NIV)

My Testimony.

During the early days of my writing for children, an adult asked, "Why don't you write for women?" I answered, "Because God has put it into my heart to write for children!"

While you are learning to recognize the Holy Spirit's leading, here is a motto that will help you when you aren't sure if you are understanding Him correctly:

"If in Doubt, Don't."

It is better to wait until you know for sure
than to rush ahead of what the Holy Spirit wants you to do.

Be comforted by this verse:

> *"For those who are _______ by the ____________ of God are the ___________________ of God."* Romans 8:14 (NIV)

5. Hymns

Singing hymns is a way to worship the Trinity. When we give thanks to God for every blessing, it helps us worship Him. When we sing about Jesus and the Holy Spirit, our heart responds with love and appreciation.

King David, the author of most of the songs in the Book of Psalms, tells us to sing.

Read the Bible verses. Then fill in the blanks.

Psalm 96:1–2 (NIV). *"Sing to the LORD a new ____________; ____________ to the LORD, all the ____________. Sing to the LORD, __________________ his name."*
(You may want to color-code these verses in brown.)

Colossians 3:16 (NIV). In the New Testament, Paul said: *"Let the message of Christ dwell among you richly as you teach and admonish one another with all wisdom through ______________, ______________, and ______________ from the Spirit, singing to God with __________________ in your hearts."*

Today's Music

Down through the centuries, Christian men and women have created songs that have proclaimed the truth of God, His Son, and the Holy Spirit. As you sing songs from a hymnal, you will worship and feel the presence of the Holy Spirit speaking to your heart.

One person you may have heard about is Fannie Crosby. Although blind at the age of six weeks, she wrote over 6000 hymns. Many of these could be sung as part of your private worship.

Perhaps you know some of these: "Praise Him! Praise Him!" "Tell Me the Story of Jesus" "To God Be the Glory." "Blessed Assurance" is my testimony.

Blessed assurance Jesus is mine!
O, what a foretaste of glory divine!
Heir of salvation, purchase of God,
Born of His Spirit, washed in His blood.
Chorus. *This is my story, this is my song,*
Praising my Savior all the day long.

What song is your testimony? Write the words here.

____

____

CHALLENGE

How the Holy Spirit Speaks to Us

Find the best word from this list to fill in the blank spaces.

Bible	**Impressions**	**Promptings**
Evangelists	**King**	**Teachers**
Feelings	**Leadings**	**Witness**
Hymns	**Pastors**	**Word**

___ ___ **S** ___ ___ ___ ___

___ ___ ___ ___ **P** ___ ___ ___ ___ ___

___ **I** ___ ___ ___

___ ___ **R** ___

___ ___ ___ ___ **I** ___ ___ ___

___ ___ **T** ___ ___ ___ ___

___ ___ ___ ___ ___ ___ ___ **S**

___ ___ **P** ___ ___ ___ ___ ___ ___ ___ ___

___ ___ ___ ___ ___ **E** ___ ___ ___ ___ ___

___ ___ **A** ___ ___ ___ ___ ___

K ___ ___ ___

___ ___ ___ ___ **S**

DISCUSSION

1. When have you felt a prompting to do something? (Like help someone, compliment a person, or read a certain Scripture.)
2. Think or talk about a time that you now recognize as the Holy Spirit leading you.

Answers on page 124

APPLICATION

1. You may want to keep a notebook (diary, journal) about when you feel the Holy Spirit speak to you. Write down any follow-up or result.
2. Learn more about Fannie Crosby by reading about her on the Internet or in an encyclopedia.
3. A Verse to Memorize. Copy the verse below on an index card. Underline or print important words (shown in bold print) in color to help you remember the verse. You may want to color-code this verse in your Bible as well.

We ***know*** *that in all* ***things***
God works *for the good of those who* ***love*** *him,*
who have been ***called*** *according to his* ***purpose****.*

Romans 8:28 (NIV), emphasis added

PRAYER

Heavenly Father,
Thank You for sending the Holy Spirit
to speak to me and show me how to live
in a way that pleases You. I want to bring
a smile to Your face, dear God.
Now that I know the ways
the Holy Spirit can speak to me,
I will be more aware of His presence and leadership.
Thank You, Lord, for the people who minister to me
(name pastor, teachers, leaders).
Please protect them, make them wise, and bless their ministry.
Please make me alive to the leadings of the Holy Spirit.
I ask all this in the name of Jesus Christ. Amen.

20

The Holy Spirit Adopts Us

Memory Verse: The Spirit you received brought about your adoption to sonship. And by him we cry, "Abba, Father."

ROMANS 8:15b (NIV)

WHAT IS ADOPTION?

An earthly adoption is when a man, woman, or couple take a child into their home. They give the family name, home, privileges, and inheritance to someone who is not their child by birth.

Adoption is common today. Couples take in children from different nationalities, making a blended family of color and languages. Perhaps you have a friend who enjoys the privileges of being adopted.

READ A PLAY

A good example of an adoption is found in the Old Testament. Let's read this play based on Exodus 2:1–8. If you have more than one person in your group or family, you can assign a different reader for each part. If not, then you can read the play yourself.

From a Lowly Hut to a Palace

CAST:

Narrator—storyteller who describes the actions and settings

Pharaoh—king of Egypt

Hatshepsut (hat-SHEP-sōōt)—daughter of Pharaoh

Jochebed (JOK-uh-bed)—Moses' mother

Miriam—sister of Moses

Scene—Palace of Pharaoh

Narrator: One day a new Egyptian king came to power. He met with his advisors about a serious concern.

Pharaoh: Look. The Hebrew people are growing in number rapidly. They are becoming very powerful. Someday they may even make war with us.

Narrator: The Egyptians made the Hebrews their slaves. Cruel slave drivers were appointed to crush them with back-breaking work. But the more the slaves were beaten down, the more they multiplied. The king gave a new order to all the people.

Pharaoh: Every boy that is born to the Hebrews must be thrown into the Nile River. Every girl is to be kept alive.

Narrator: A Levite couple, Amram and Jochebed, had two children: Miriam and Aaron. Jochebed became pregnant again and gave birth to a son.

Jochebed Oh, Amram! What a beautiful boy we have. I will nurse him and hide him as long as I can.

Narrator: She hid their baby boy for three months. Then his cries grew louder and could be heard outside their home.

Miriam: Mother, what we will do now?

Jochebed: I will cover a basket with tar and pitch so it will not leak. I will place your brother in the basket. Then we will put the basket among the tall reeds along the bank of the Nile River. Miriam, you will hide nearby and watch to see what happens to him.

Narrator: Soon Hatshepsut, daughter of Pharaoh, came down to bathe in the river. Several attendants came along to protect her.

When she spied the basket, she called out to a maiden.

Hatshepsut: Look! There is a basket stuck in the reeds. Please bring it to me.

Narrator: Pharaoh's daughter opened the basket. She saw a crying baby boy, and her heart melted with sympathy.

Hatshepsut: Oh my! This is one of the Hebrew babies.

Narrator: Miriam hurried from her hiding place.

Miriam: Shall I go and find a Hebrew woman to nurse the baby for you?

Hatshepsut: Yes! That's a good idea. Go find a nurse for him!

Narrator: Miriam ran and got her mother. Jochebed came quickly.

Hatshepsut: Here, take this baby and nurse him for me. I will pay you for your services.

Narrator: So Jochebed took her son home and nursed him. When the boy grew older, she took him to the palace and gave him to Pharaoh's daughter.

Hatshepsut adopted the boy, and he became her son. She named him Moses because she took him out of the water.

—The End—

THE HOLY SPIRIT ADOPTS YOU

Because of God's grace and your faith, you are adopted into the family of God. How can you know this is true? Find proof in these verses.

Read the Bible verses. Then fill in the blanks.

Romans 8:16 (NIV). *"The Spirit himself ____________________ with our spirit that we are ________ ____________________."*

John 1:12 (NIV). *"Yet to all who did receive him, to those who believed in his name, he gave the right to _____________ ________________ ____ ________."*

2 Corinthians 6:18 (NIV). *"I will be a ___________ to you, and you will be my _______ and _______________, says the Lord _________________."*

Galatians 4:4–5 (NIV). *"God sent his _______, born of a woman,…to redeem those under the law, that we might receive________________ to sonship."*

1 Peter 1:3–4 (NIV). *"Praise be to the God and ______________ of our Lord Jesus Christ! In his great mercy he has given us new birth into a living hope through the ___________________ of Jesus Christ from the dead, and into an _____________________ that can never perish, spoil or ___________."*

CHALLENGE

The Rewards of Being Adopted

Just as an adopted child benefits from becoming part of an earthly family, we receive wonderful rewards from becoming part of God's family.

Follow these three steps to learn more about what to expect as a member of God's family!

1. Look up the Reference. (Verses are from the NIV Bible.)
2. Match it with the Verse. (Words may not be exact depending on the translation of your Bible.)
3. Match with the Reward.

Draw the icon from the first box anywhere in the matching boxes.

Reference	Verse	Reward
Romans 8:17 	*"When you believed, you were marked in him with a seal, the promised Holy Spirit...*	*And we eagerly await a Savior...who...will transform our lowly bodies so that they will be like his glorious body."*
1 John 3:1 	*"Has not God chosen those who are poor in the eyes of the world...*	*who is a deposit guaranteeing our inheritance until the redemption of those who are God's possession."*
Philippians 3:20–21 	*"See what great love the Father has lavished on us...*	*to be rich in faith and to inherit the kingdom he promised those who love him?"*
James 2:5 	*"Now if we are children, then we are heirs —*	*that we should be called children of God!"*
Ephesians 1:13b–14 	*"But our citizenship is in heaven.*	*heirs of God and co-heirs with Christ."*

Answers on page 124

DISCUSSION

1. Think or talk about how God can take a negative experience and turn it into a positive. Use Moses as an example.
2. Name one thing that you have learned from this book about the Holy Spirit. How has your walk with Jesus improved because of what you have learned? What questions do you still have?

APPLICATION

1. Do you have any friends who are adopted? Encourage them because they have been "chosen." Perhaps you could tell them of your adoption into God's family.
2. A Verse to Memorize. Copy the verse below on an index card. Underline or print important words (shown in bold print) in color to help you remember the verse. You may want to color-code this verse in your Bible as well.

"For I ***know*** *the* ***plans*** *I have for you,"*
declares *the* LORD, *"plans to* ***prosper*** *you*
and ***not*** *to* ***harm*** *you,*
plans to ***give*** *you* ***hope*** *and a* ***future****."*

Jeremiah 29:11 (NIV), emphasis added

PRAYER

Heavenly Father,
You are great and worthy of praise.
You are loving, kind, and merciful.
Thank You for adopting me as Your own child.
That is such a comforting thought.
I feel safe, loved, and protected.
I'm so glad to be part of the family of God.
Thank You, God, Jesus, and the Holy Spirit
for making this possible.
In the saving name of Jesus, amen.

ANSWERS

Page 11:

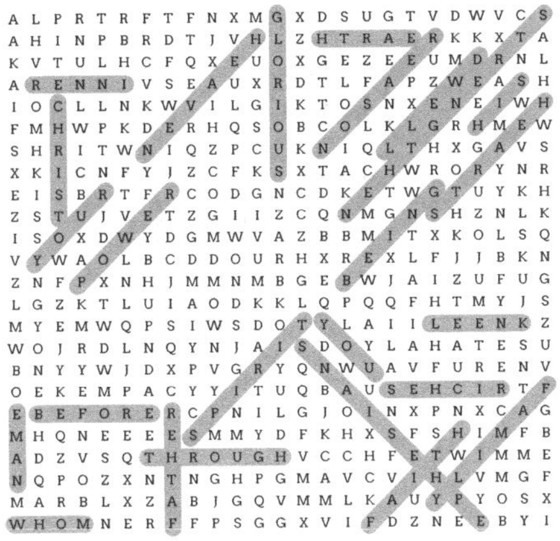

Page 31

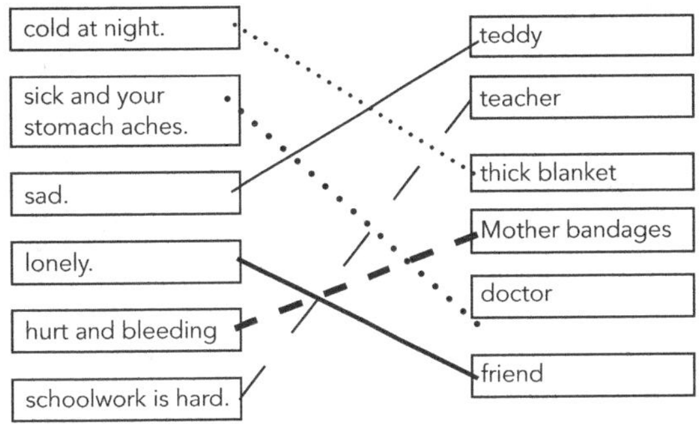

Page 14:

Page 38:

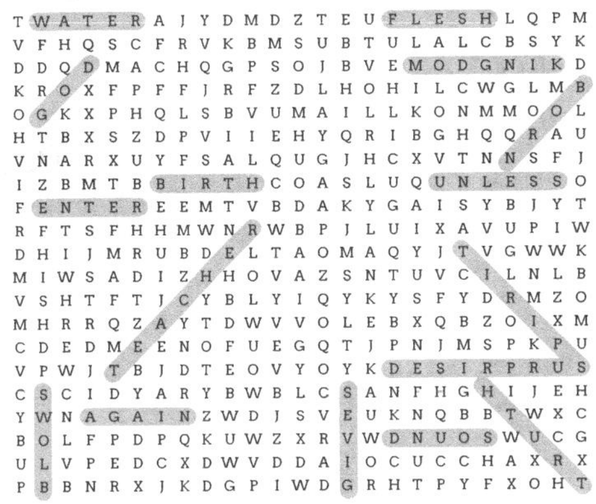

Page 21:

Nine Fruits of the Spirit

1. Peace
2. Gentleness
3. Love
4. Kindness
5. Joy
6. Faithfulness

Page 15:

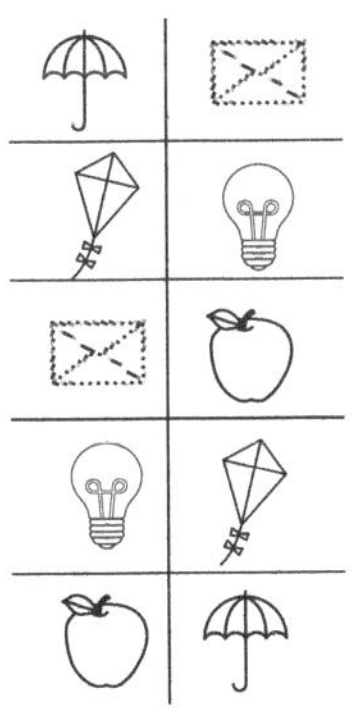

Page 22:

7. Self-Control
8. Goodness
9a. Forbearance (NIV)
9b. Longsuffering (NKJV)
9c. Patience (NLT)

From: Galatians 5:22–23

Page 39:

B
D
G
A
E
H
C
F

Page 20:

How Can You Honor God?

1. Serve one another humbly in love.
2. Love your neighbor as yourself.
3. Walk by the Spirit.
4. Led by the Spirit.
5. Live by the Spirit.
6. Keep in step with the Spirit.

Page 28:

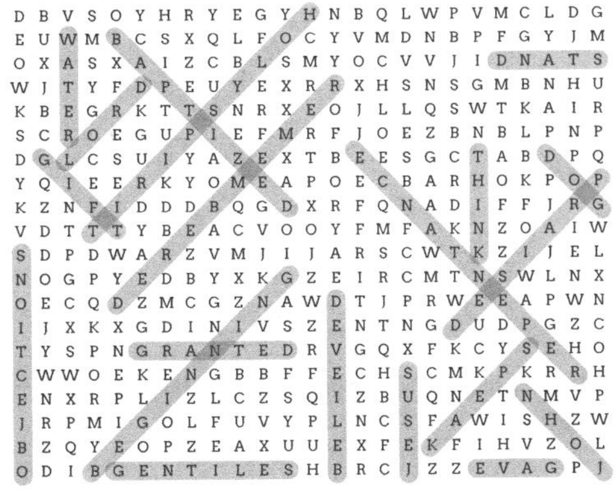

Page 43:

Doors Open; Doors Close

1. Barnabas and Saul
2. Selucia and Cyprus
3. province of Asia
4. would not let them
5. Leave Jerusalem
6. Take courage

Page 44:

Luke 1:26–28
Virgin Mary
God sent angel Gabriel

Matthew 2:12
The Magi
God warned in a dream

Matthew 2:19
Joseph
An angel of the Lord appeared in a dream

Luke 4:1
Jesus
Led by the Spirit into the wilderness

Acts 8:39
Phillip
Spirit of the Lord

Acts 9:10
Ananias
In a vision, the Lord called

Acts 10:3
Cornelius
In a vision, an angel of God appeared

Acts 10:13
Peter
A Voice spoke

Acts 13:1–2
Prophets & Teachers
Holy Spirit gave instructions

Acts 22:17–18
Paul
In a trance, he saw the Lord speaking

Page 48:

1. The joy of the Lord is your strength.
2. A cheerful heart is good medicine.
3. A happy heart makes the face cheerful.

Page 49:

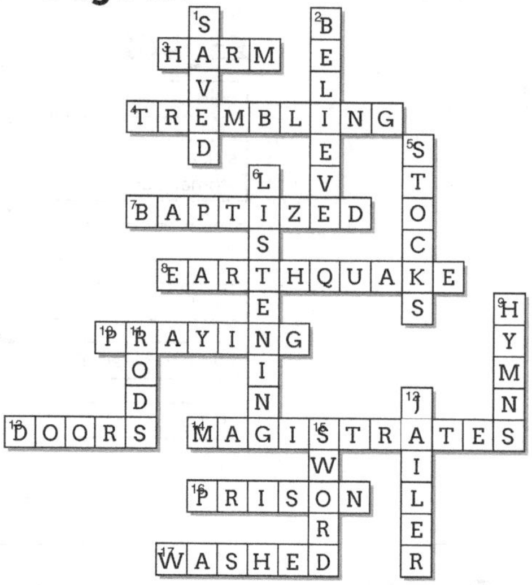

Page 55:

FAITH
TR**U**TH
BE**L**T
SA**L**VATION

BRE**A**STPLATE
SPI**R**IT
HEL**M**ET
RIGHTE**O**USNESS
P**R**AYERS

W**O**RD
FEET

GOSPEL
SW**O**RD
SHIEL**D**

Page 61:

Q	X	T	O	Z	Q	X	Z	T	H	E	Q	X
Z	Q	Z	P	E	R	S	O	N	Z	Q	X	Z
W	H	O	Z	X	Q	Z	X	Q	Q	X	Z	Q
X	Q	X	Q	Z	X	P	L	E	A	S	E	S
Q	Z	Z	H	I	M	Q	Z	X	Z	Q	X	Z
Z	G	O	D	Q	Z	X	G	I	V	E	S	X
X	Q	W	I	S	D	O	M	Z	Q	Z	Q	Z
Q	Z	X	Q	K	N	O	W	L	E	D	G	E
Z	A	N	D	Q	Z	X	Q	X	Z	Q	Z	X
X	Q	H	A	P	P	I	N	E	S	S	X	Q
E	C	C	L	E	S	I	A	S	T	E	S	Z
X	Z	C	H	A	P	T	E	R	X	2	Q	X
Z	Q	X	Z	V	E	R	S	E	Z	2	6	Q

To the person who **pleases** Him.
1. Wisdom
2. Knowledge
3. Happiness

Ecclesiastes 2:26

Page 64:

Page 66:

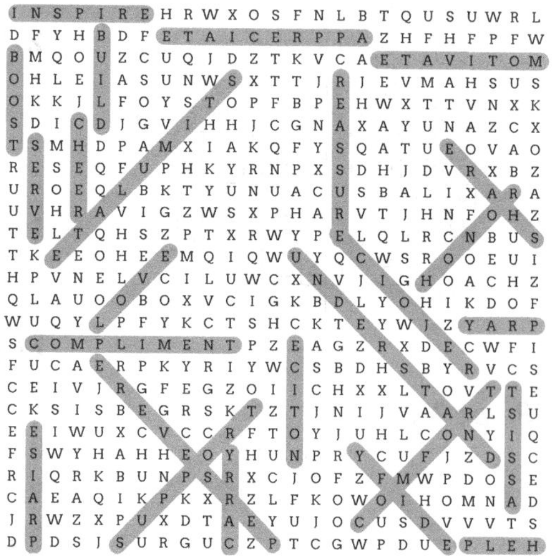

Page 69:

***V. 6** Prophesying
***V. 7** Teaching
***V. 8** Encourage
***V. 8** Show Mercy
#V. 9 Hospitality
#V. 11 Speaks
***V. 7** Serving
***V. 8** Giving
***V. 8** Lead

Page 74:

Page 76:

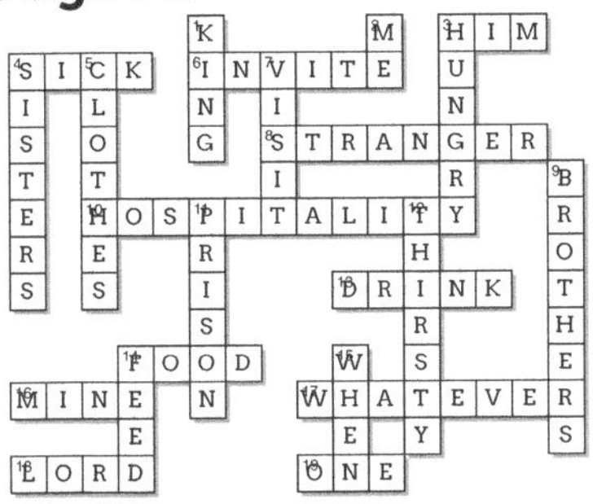

Page 79:

NIV is first answer; if different, NKJV is in italics

1. teach you all things
2. remind you of everything I have said to you

   bring to your remembrance all things
3. testify about me
4. guide you into all truth
5. speak only what he hears

   whatever he hears he will speak
6. tell you what is to come

   tell you things to come
7. glorify me
8. make known to you

   declare it to you
9. marked in him with a seal

   sealed with the Holy Spirit
10. guaranteeing our inheritance

    is the guarantee of our inheritance

Page 80:

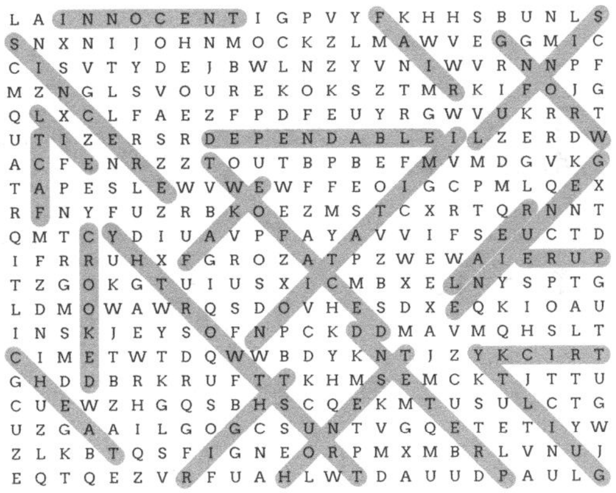

Page 81:

Truth	Falsehood
Dependable	Cheat
Pure	Lie
Fact	Crooked
Real	Pretend
Fair	Fake
Right	Sinful
Genuine	Guilty
Honest	Tricky
Innocent	Imitation
Sincere	Two-faced
Trustworthy	Wrong

Page 85:

D Anger

D Rage

A Lying, telling falsehoods

B Stealing

F Telling dirty or coarse jokes

E Greed

G Selfishness

D Bitterness

C Unwholesome talk (verbally tearing one another down)

D Brawling, fighting

E Sexual misconduct

F Obscenity (bad language)

Page 86

(Possible Suggestions)

A. amiable, admiring, accepting, attentive

B. big-hearted, brave, a booster

C. calm, cool, cheerful, courteous, considerate

D. devoted, dependable, dedicated

E. encouraging, enthusiastic

F. forgiving, faithful, friendly, fair, firm

G. gentle, generous, gracious

H. honest, helpful, humble

I. inspiring, impartial

J. just, jovial

K. kind, kindhearted

L. loving, likeable, loyal

M. merciful, magnanimous, memorizer of Bible verses

N. nice, nonviolent, natural

O. outgoing, obedient, optimistic

P. peaceful, polite, positive, prayerful, patient

R. respectful, reverent, reliable, realistic, reader of the Bible

S. sincere, supportive, sympathetic, sensitive

T. thoughtful, truthful, tactful, tenderhearted

U. uplifting, understanding, unwavering, upbeat

W. well-mannered, wholesome language, welcoming

Y. young-at-heart

Z. zealous

Page 91:

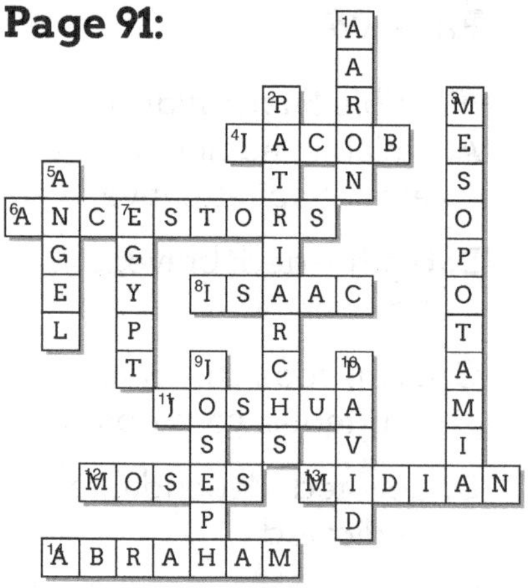

Page 93:

Page 99:

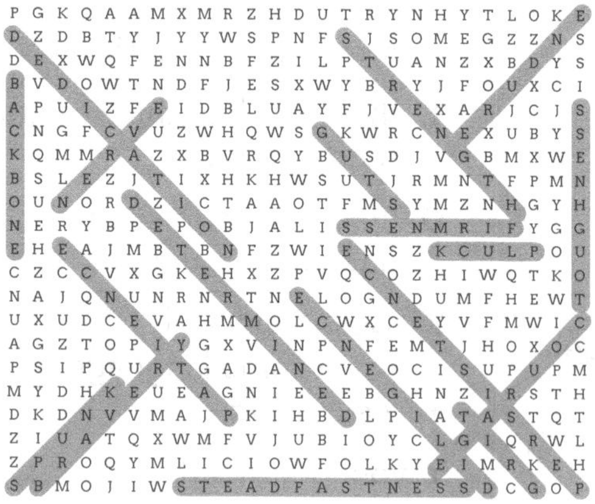

Page 101:

1. power, spirit
2. produces perseverance
3. gives me strength
4. can endure it

Page 105:

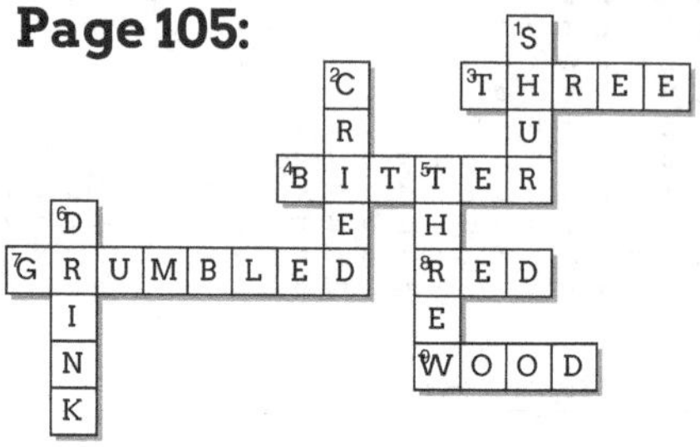

Page 108:

Prayers of Jesus Christ

1. PRAYED YOUR FAITH FAIL
2. BELIEVE ME
3. FORGIVE THEM KNOW WHAT DOING
4. SAVE GOD LIVES INTERCEDE THEM

Page 114:

PA**S**TORS
PROM**P**TING
B**I**BLE
WO**R**D
FEEL**I**NGS
WI**T**NESS

LEADING**S**
IM**P**RESSIONS
EVANG**E**LISTS
TE**A**CHERS
KING
HYMN**S**

Page 119: